More Recipes for Your Bread Machine Bakery

ALSO BY RICHARD W. LANGER

The After-Dinner Gardening Book
Grow It!
Grow It Indoors
The Joy of Camping
The Bread Machine Bakery Book

More Recipes for Your Bread Machine Bakery

Richard W. Langer

Illustrations by Susan McNeill

LITTLE, BROWN AND COMPANY ❖ BOSTON ❖ TORONTO ❖ LONDON

FIRST EDITION

Library of Congress Cataloging-in-Publication Data

Langer, Richard W.
    More recipes for your bread machine bakery / Richard W. Langer;
illustrations by Susan McNeill. — 1st ed.
        p.   cm.
    Includes index.
    ISBN 0-316-51390-3
    1. Bread.   2. Automatic bread machines.   I. Title.
TX769.L275   1992
641.8'15 — dc20   92-25406

10   9   8   7   6   5   4   3   2   1

MV-NY

PUBLISHED SIMULTANEOUSLY IN CANADA BY LITTLE, BROWN
& COMPANY (CANADA) LIMITED

PRINTED IN THE UNITED STATES OF AMERICA

To Susan —
great editor, wonderful illustrator,
and the best of wives

Contents

More Recipes for Your Bread Machine Bakery

1 · The Aroma Made Me Do It

BAKING IS ONE OF THOSE SIMPLE PLEASURES, like fishing, that never really was all that simple. It inspires visions of a sunny country kitchen where a comfortable sort of cat lies curled on the braided rug and a great ceramic bowl of rising dough reposes on the warming shelf at the back of a wood stove, filling the air with the fragrance of cinnamon and yeast. What is absent from this picture is the kneading of the dough between risings that requires one's presence at least intermittently for the four to six hours needed to complete the loaf, the telephone interruptions, and finding the dough overflowing its warm confines on one's return from a dash to the mall three hours later than expected, not to mention the screech of the cat when its tail is stepped on as one hurls oneself into the kitchen to rescue the overextended bread.

In short, reality and the vision do not coincide. Furthermore, as is so often the case these days, the shimmering media image suffusing us doesn't help matters at all. We are promised convenience, sliced bread, fresh softness you can squeeze — in exchange for which we have lost flavor, variety, and the pleasure of bread as something more than a wrapper for other foods.

And so specialty bakers have come to the fore. In the last decade or so, whole-grain loaves in all manner of free-form shapes along with ethnic and festive breads of every variety have once more become available. One of the virtues of bread as a food, after all, has always been its diversity.

Home baking too is reviving, for, as many people are either remembering or discovering for the first time, there's nothing quite like the pleasure of a loaf of bread hot from the oven, its aroma pervading the entire house — if one has the time to devote to its making. It is this proviso that Japanese marketing executives applying their skills to consumer goods perceived as a sure opportunity. The result was the bread machine.

Unfortunately, the recipe booklets included with the various makes of this device really don't demonstrate the full potential of the machine. Considering that the engineers who designed it grew up in a rice- rather than a bread-based culture, and considering that the previous sallies of Japanese sales divisions into popular expository writing were focused primarily on manuals for such devices as VCRs and personal computers, this weakness is not surprising. What is surprising is how good and how varied the loaves coaxed from a bread machine can be, given the right recipes.

Some of the diversity, in fact, can be attributed to the machines themselves. Different makes and models produce somewhat different breads from a single recipe. For instance, the instant-mashed-potato bread recipe in this book results in a loaf with a more open texture, a chewier consistency, and a smaller size when baked in a National or Panasonic machine than it has when made in a Hitachi. A Hitachi-made loaf of the same bread is larger, but a little drier and crustier. Each loaf, however, has a worthy texture and taste of its own.

Speaking of things larger, the first bread machines all produced one-pound loaves of bread. Certain of the newer machines, such as the National and Panasonic large-loaf models, make an oblong pound-and-a-half loaf. The Hitachi can also bake a large-size loaf, although it will be a tall bread rather than an oblong one. I have included recipes for the big loaves as well as for the small in this book, but on the whole I find that most machines make a bread more even in texture and consistent in quality in the original one-pound size. Considering how easy it is to make fresh bread with a bread machine, I'll take small loaves baked more often over large loaves with leftovers.

The major functional difference between the various machines lies in the power of their kneading blades. DAK and Welbilt models do not deal well with a heavy dough, for instance. If these machines seem to be struggling with the task of kneading a bread, barely turning the dough around in the baking pan, you may need to add a bit of extra liquid, a tablespoonful at a time.

Two new extended baking cycles have been added to the National and Panasonic machines now on the market. One, for whole-wheat breads, allows more time for nonwhite bread doughs to rise. Since this setting is not an option on many of the other bread machines, however, all the recipes for whole-wheat and multigrain breads in this book have been created to work with either the rapid or the regular baking mode of your bread machine.

The second new setting was designed to facilitate a crisp crust on a bread. Essentially all this setting does is to extend the time allowed for rising even further. Yet most of the snappiness of a crust still depends on the ingredients used and the oven environment during baking. No bread machine yet devised will yield the brittle shell of a true French baguette that sends shards flying across the room when a piece of the loaf is broken off. That bread can be baked properly only in an oven misted with cold water.

The microelectronics underlying today's bread machines could make possible the baking of a true baguette in tomorrow's electronic oven, however. The only modification needed would be the addition of a water reservoir and a misting mechanism. The water reservoir would add but fractionally to the cost of the machine. The mister, being a mechanical mechanism, might add as much as 20 percent to the price. Still, those two refinements plus a separate compartment to allow for the delayed release of such things as raisins, nuts, and creamy fillings during the last kneading cycle (so that these embellishments would remain whole rather than being homogenized in the dough during the kneading process) are improvements one can hope the electronic ovens of the future will incorporate.

Meanwhile, all the breads in this book can be baked in any of the machines currently on the market — with two caveats. First, the heavier doughs, as mentioned, will probably need some extra liquid if they're to be kneaded in a DAK or a Welbilt. Quite simply, these machines are somewhat underpowered. Second, machines like the large Panasonic model featuring the oblong, more traditional loaf-shaped pans need a bit of initial supervision before they are left to their job. Thick or sticky doughs are sometimes not picked up from the corners of the rectangular pan by the kneading blade. Keep handy a rubber spatula with which to scrape down the sides of the pan about five or ten minutes into the preliminary mixing cycle. However, the lid on a machine featuring a separate container for leavening should be opened either before or after the yeast has been dispensed, not during that operation, for obvious reasons.

Whichever machine you have, don't be afraid to experiment with it. Bread machines afford one the opportunity to bake not only home-made loaves of countless traditional varieties, but new and different ones never made before. True, one will encounter the occasional disaster. I particularly remember an experiment of mine with a blue-corn bread, the failed results of which, a steaming, oozing blue blob whose closeup on videotape could have been used in a remake of *It Came from Outer Space,* still rested on a cooling rack in the center of our kitchen table when in walked Tanya, our mature high-school senior, with her date. I don't recall his name, perhaps because he never came back. . . .

Then there was the time, during a singularly frenetic baking session, when I ascended from the basement with a couple of half gallons of ice cream retrieved from the big freezer downstairs to replenish the smaller one in the kitchen refrigerator. As I walked by Revell's room, that twelve-year-old, not too busy building his nth balsa-wood sailboat for the pond to notice my passage, looked up and said, "You're not."

"Not what?"

"Going to make ice-cream bread."

"Oh, come on . . ."

"Well," Tanya chimed in from behind the easel in her room to which she was tacking filaments of lace in an intricate pattern for her graduation dress, "why not? How about baked Alaska, Dad?"

I left hanging the reference to that namesake of the forty-ninth state and helped myself to some ice cream in the hot kitchen, where three machines were at the moment busy churning the dough for refried bean, Bulgarian cheese, and beer bread, respectively. Ice-cream bread, indeed!

All the same, experimenting is part of the fun of owning a bread machine, and for each failure there's a spectacular success. Use the recipes in this book to familiarize yourself with the range of nutritious and flavorsome breads you can bake in your electronic oven. But don't stop there. By all means do go on to create your own personalized loaves.

2 · Sugar and Spice and Flour and Rice

ONE OF THE ADVANTAGES of home baking with a bread machine is that you know what goes into every loaf. You can accommodate family whims and dietary needs or restrictions, use nothing but the finest and freshest ingredients, and rest assured that you are truly producing the staff of life.

As bread machines have proliferated, so have specialized flours and mixes catering to their use. The recipes in this book, however, are designed primarily around standard flours commonly available in the supermarket. Where the occasional rarer ingredient is called for, it will be found either in health-food stores or from the mail-order suppliers listed at the back of the book.

The special bread flour found increasingly on grocery shelves as bread machines multiply is a high-gluten flour, containing more of this protein than ordinary flour can boast. Gluten is what adds elasticity and stretch to a batch of dough, trapping the gas released by the fermenting yeast and enabling the bread to rise. All wheat flour contains some gluten, however, and in working with any of the recipes presented here, I've found no need for the special bread flour on the market. In some cases, in fact, the extra gluten in bread flour causes a dough to overflow its pan unpredictably.

This is not to discourage you altogether from using bread flour if that's what you have handy. I simply suggest care in substituting it for regular flour in a recipe.

By preference, I do use unbleached rather than bleached flour. The bleaching process used to whiten flour involves chlorination, while unbleached flour is lightened naturally through aging. Having always used unbleached flour in my baking, I could see no reason to switch merely because I'd acquired a bread machine. But bleached flour works just as well, so if it's the flour of your choice or more readily available in your area, don't hesitate to substitute it for the unbleached variety.

There's a raft of other flours, among them whole-wheat, rye, barley, buckwheat, millet, semolina, and brown rice, used for the recipes in this book. Many of these flours contain perishable oils from the germ, or heart, of the grain and are best kept refrigerated if you're going to have them around for more than a month or so, as otherwise they can spoil and lend a bitter taste to your bread. This isn't much of a problem in our corner of New England except in the summertime. However, if you live in a warmer region, refrigeration year-round is a good idea.

Speaking of refrigeration, most books on baking will tell you that the ingredients for a loaf of bread should be at room temperature before being used. I've always abided by this axiom myself. But given the premise that the principal attraction of a bread machine is its convenience, the idea of waiting half an hour or so for the eggs and milk and flour and what have you to warm up before starting one's baking seems contradictory to the mission of the machine. So, modifying my habitual routine, I've baked all the breads in this book with any refrigerated ingredients taken straight from their storage spot as needed. It's worked out just fine. By the time the machine's kneading blade has performed its initial mixing ritual, the ingredients have become quite warm and cozy. The one exception, a large cold block of butter, I've dealt with simply by cutting the bar into small pieces before adding it to my batter.

However, if you store rarely used specialty flours in the freezer, a practice well worth adopting, let them warm up half an hour or so before using them. Starters frozen in premeasured batches need more time, as much as three to four hours, to thaw, for in order to do their job properly they need to be bubbly when incorporated into the dough they are expected to leaven. This natural thawing produces more flavorsome bread, to my mind. However, it is possible to save time by zapping a batch of starter in your microwave, using the method recommended in your machine's instructions for thawing bread dough. Stir in a tablespoon of flour as soon as you take the starter from the microwave, and make sure it's revived enough to be bubbly before using it to bake your bread.

Each of the specialty flours adds its own characteristic taste and texture to the bread in which it's used. Whole wheat, as the name implies, includes the entire wheat kernel. It also contains a lot of bran, which contributes healthful dietary fiber. The germ and the bran are what give this flour its distinctive light brown color. But these heavier components also slow the rise of the whole-wheat, as opposed to white-flour, dough. That's why some of the newer bread machines have a whole-wheat mode among their settings.

The whole-wheat setting extends the dough's rising time so that the heavier mixes can catch up with their airier counterparts. However, a lot of machines do not provide this option, and even those that do retain the shorter rising period for their rapid-bake cycle. So, to make life simpler, most of the breads in this book have been baked on the short cycle, spanning roughly three hours. The regular cycle takes around four hours, the whole-wheat setting five, and the crisp mode available on a few machines seven hours from start to finish. Generally the only noticeable difference in the loaf these settings yield is that it's a bit taller and more open in texture.

Bran, the protective coating surrounding the kernels of grains, for years announced its presence in breads mostly in the coffee-counter muffins carrying its name. Bran as a cereal sold listlessly from the grocer's shelves. Then, in the late eighties, the American Medical Association released a study indicating that a high-fiber diet including oat bran might help reduce blood cholesterol. Suddenly there wasn't enough oat bran procurable at any price.

The craze is over now, but bran is still a good ingredient for bread, adding texture and flavor as well as nutrition and roughage. I prefer unprocessed wheat bran to oat bran. The wheat variety has more fiber and better flavor than the oat does.

Semolina, traditional in pasta, is also excellent in bread. Milled from protein-rich durum wheat with only the aforementioned bran layer removed, it contributes a golden hue and a silky texture to a loaf.

Use rye flour in your bread, and your loaf will maintain a low profile, dense and compact, regardless of the setting you use in baking it, for this flour contains little gluten. The higher the proportion of rye in a recipe, then, the smaller the loaf will be. But that's the way rye breads have always been, fine textured — and tasty indeed.

Pumpernickel is simply a coarse grade of rye. It contains a great deal of bran and makes for a loaf even denser than one produced with the medium rye found on supermarket shelves. If a recipe calls for pumpernickel and you can't locate this flour locally, you can substitute rye for it, or you can do as I do and order it by mail.

Mention barley, and I think of beef and barley soup, a dish I toss into the same category as I do okra, both being somewhat slimy and not favorites of mine. But barley does make a good bread, nutty and very fine in texture.

Millet, as I keep insisting to the kids, really isn't birdseed. True, your standard modern cage-bird mix is full of its tiny yellow spheres, but millet has been a staple of the human race for millenniums. At one time it was more popular than rice in China, and it is still a major food crop in Africa. Whole millet adds a lovely crunch to bread.

Rice is the "daily bread" of more than half the population of the earth. It is central particularly to the diet of peoples in the tropics. Rice and bread are rarely found in each other's company, as we tend to eat but one starchy food at a time. But rice flour gives bread a silky quality. It's also a valuable ingredient in gluten-free loaves for those who can't eat regular bread because of gluten intolerance. Even baking whole rice into a loaf results in a surprisingly good bread, as our family discovered quite by accident.

Corn is normally regarded as a vegetable, and corn on the cob is probably America's favorite in that category of foods. But in fact corn is a grain. As cornmeal, it lends an agreeably gritty texture to bread. However, a pure cornmeal batter in a bread machine rises to at best a rather dry and crumbly loaf. When you experiment with this grain, use it as an adjunct to wheat flour, not by itself.

Like cornmeal and bran, oatmeal adds texture and a pleasant roughness to the breads in which it's used. Steel-cut oats, the ones common to Scottish and Irish oatmeal, are the least processed form of this cereal outside of whole oat groats. The oats have been chopped by sharp steel blades to reduce the cereal's normal cooking time from a couple of hours to somewhere in the neighborhood of forty minutes. Because no heat is generated by the blades, steel-cut oats are supposed to retain more flavor and nourishment than rolled oats. They add a lot of texture to a bread and are worth experimenting with.

Rolled oats, the ones most common in this country, have been softened slightly by steam and then flattened between steel rollers. Quick oats are rolled a little thinner, and instant oatmeal is squashed paper-thin and then dehydrated. All can be used in breads, but the instant oatmeal adds the least texture and nutrition. I don't recommend it in the recipes in this book, simply because a bread machine can handle any of the other, more nutritious forms in which this cereal is found.

Potatoes, though neither a grain nor a cereal, are often added to bread to lighten the loaf. Potato breads are widespread in central Europe, as are the robust, earthy breads utilizing buckwheat. However, outside of the United States, where it early became associated with the prodigious pancake stack, buckwheat is more prevalent in its cooked whole hulled form, kasha.

Eggs are a supplementary leavening agent. They help to make a loaf wonderfully light. But they also predispose it to premature staleness. A real egg bread goes noticeably stale within a couple of hours. That's why being able to have a fresh loaf hot from the electronic oven just when it's wanted is a real plus for the bread machine. It's also why extra moisture in the form of oil or butter is usually part and parcel of an egg loaf.

The primary leavening agent in most breads is yeast. Quick breads are leavened with baking powder, and it's possible to make them in a bread machine, although most manufacturers of these devices recommend merely mixing the batter in the machine and then pouring the result into a regular bread pan to bake in a standard oven. That seems to me to defeat the main purpose of using a bread machine in the first place.

Where the bread machines really prove their mettle is in so capably, reliably, and effortlessly handling the lengthier task of producing yeast breads. Yeast is available in the traditional fresh cake or in dried form, either as what is called active dry yeast or in a newer rapid-rise variant. But because the old-fashioned yeast cakes are both more difficult to find and not accommodated by bread machines having a separate yeast dispenser, and because I've found the new rapid-rise version unpredictable in the machines, I've adopted regular active dry yeast as my leavening of choice.

Which brand of yeast to use is a question I'm often asked, and the answer to that question is bound to be subjective. Yeasts do vary, and people tend to use what has served them well in the past. Some bakers swear that imported European yeasts work best in bread machines. Others find that whatever is available on the supermarket shelf, which usually turns out to be Fleischmann's or Red Star, suits them fine. As it so happens, I use Red Star, simply because it's the one yeast I can purchase in bulk, and I go through pounds and pounds of yeast when I'm developing and refining the recipes for a book.

Yeast consumes the carbohydrates in a bread batter and converts them into carbon dioxide gas, which in turn expands the dough, giving the finished loaf its characteristic open, airy texture. To provide the yeast with plenty of carbohydrates to draw on, sugars are often included in a bread recipe. White sugar, brown sugar, corn syrup, honey, molasses, and barley malt syrup all have their place in bread making. Besides providing sustenance for the yeast, they add tenderness and flavor to a loaf.

The various sweeteners can usually be substituted one for another. However, if you use, say, brown sugar in place of molasses, then you may need to increase slightly the amount of liquid called for in the recipe.

Also, it's quite possible to have too much of a good thing. I've experimented with a number of recipes using flavorings such as jam or chutney, and unless I used so little of these ingredients that their flavor didn't really come through, I ended up with so much sugar in the dough that the yeast was overpowered and the dough wouldn't rise properly.

But spices and herbs won't overpower the yeast with sugar, no matter how much of them you add to a dough. So they can be used liberally to flavor a loaf. Of course, there is a limit to what the taste buds will accept, although this point of no return varies greatly from individual to individual.

The proportions of herbs and spices to the other ingredients in the recipes in this book are pretty much middle of the road, and you can add to or subtract from the quantities listed to the point of doubling or halving them without affecting the loaves as a whole. Fresh herbs can also be substituted for dried ones, and dried for fresh. However, if you substitute fresh chopped onions for the dehydrated minced variety or for onion flakes, you'll have to add a lot more to achieve the same degree of oniony flavor. You'll also have to reduce the amount of liquid called for in the recipe by one to two tablespoons. Onions are 99 percent water.

The particular liquid in a recipe affects the quality of the bread considerably. Water, vegetable broths, and other nondairy liquids tend to foster a crispier crust and a chewier crumb. Milk encourages a softer crust and a more tender crumb. The richer the milk, the more tender the bread. Cream, cottage cheese, and buttermilk yield particularly tender loaves, as does that no-no in today's cholesterol-conscious world, butter.

I suspect we're overreacting in our dietary restrictions with our focus on low-cholesterol dining. Moderation in all things is surely commendable, but we're apt to discover in a decade or so that insufficient cholesterol is responsible for some new health peril not yet foreseen. Such are the swings of history in most things, including medical "advances." However, for those who do wish to follow an austere anti-cholesterol diet, canola oil can be substituted almost without exception for the butter or other fats listed in any of the recipes in this book. The one place where I would urge the home bread maker to stay with the ingredient listed is where olive oil is called for. Not only is the olive oil cholesterol free, but its flavor adds a lot to a bread as well.

Almost all the ingredients used in this book can be found at your local supermarket or gourmet shop. Failing that, try a health-food store, or order by mail from the sources listed at the back of this book.

3 · The Bountiful Bread Basket

ONE OF THE VERY REAL BENEFITS of a bread machine is the wide variety of loaves it makes possible without lengthy preparation. Often the selection from the supermarket or even the local bakery isn't terribly comprehensive, no matter how many shelves it occupies, and time, apportioned among too many other things, doesn't permit the hours of devotion to home baking that it once did.

The variety in the breads your machine can yield isn't visual, I'll grant you. Most of the loaves look distressingly similar if the picture conjured up in the mind's eye is drawn from memories of round rough-textured peasant breads and long woven holiday braids sparkling with currants or pearl sugar. The apricot loaf from the bread machine will have the same shape as the barley loaf, right down to the longitudinal ridges on the opposing sides left by the undulated pan. But the contents are capable of almost infinite variation, inviting experimentation.

On the other hand, sometimes nothing but the basic, primitive thing will do. One longs for a slice of simple whole-wheat toast for breakfast, or a good plain sandwich bread, or a leftover crust of some herby loaf with which to make the stuffing for a Sunday-dinner chicken. These are the breads one bakes over and over again, adding the occasional unusual loaf for accent.

Buttermilk Whole-Wheat Bread

Buttermilk is one of those old-fashioned farmstead ingredients that aren't used all that often in cooking anymore. But it's still readily available in many supermarkets, and it contributes exceptional tenderness and taste to a loaf of bread. It's a particularly fitting choice of liquid in whole-grain breads, where it adds extra loft as well as flavor.

If for some reason you have difficulty finding buttermilk in your area, put two tablespoons of yogurt or sour cream into a measuring cup and stir in enough milk to give you a level cupful of liquid. From a baking point of view, the combination is a reasonable substitute for buttermilk. Some stores also carry dried buttermilk for reconstituting if demand is not sufficient to keep the fresh product on the shelves.

SMALL

1 cup buttermilk

2 tablespoons canola oil

1 tablespoon unsulphured m͜lasses

1¾ cups whole-wheat flour

½ cup unbleached all-purpose flour

¼ to 1 teaspoon salt to taste

1½ teaspoons active dry yeast

LARGE

1¾ cups buttermilk

3 tablespoons canola oil

2 tablespoons unsulphured molasses

3 cups whole-wheat flour

¾ cup unbleached all-purpose flour

½ to 1½ teaspoons salt to taste

2 teaspoons active dry yeast

Pour the buttermilk into your bread machine baking pan and add the canola oil and molasses, unless the instructions that came with the model you have specify that the yeast is to be placed in the bottom of the pan first thing, in which case these ingredients should be added after the dry ones. Measure in the whole-wheat and all-purpose flours, the salt, and the yeast, spooning the leavening into its own dispenser if a separate container is provided for it on your machine.

Use the rapid-bake setting on your machine for this loaf.

French Sandwich Bread

French bread brings to mind those long, thin baguettes of cinematographic and novelistic allure a couple of which I would tuck under my arm each morning to transport from the *boulangerie* in Restinclières, one of those tiny villages that dot the south of France, to the small stone farm cottage at the outskirts of town that was our home for one memorable spring. Like most patrons of the *boulangerie,* I would break off a piece of the bread to nibble on my stroll. Rarely did more than a loaf and a half make it home. Often there remained but one loaf, which occasioned another walk before lunch.

Then on Tuesday and Thursday afternoons, a large white van proclaiming itself to be a mobile *charcuterie* and featuring a wide array of cheeses along with its many pâtés and sausages would ring its bell outside the cottage, and at least once a week we would treat ourselves to a substantial slab of Roquefort, which made of a buttered baguette a delectable feast. And so I would take yet another stroll to the bakery to pick up yet more baguettes.

But there's a whole other side to French bread. Among the loaves not so well known abroad is *pain de mie,* a popular sandwich loaf, square as befits its purpose, baked in a special pan with a sliding cover. As the dough rises, the cover keeps it from expanding freely. The result is the traditionally shaped fine-textured sandwich loaf equally brown on all sides.

I tried to achieve this effect in the Hitachi bread machine that doubles as a rice cooker, not to mention a jam maker, and thus has a lid for its pan. But the results were unpredictable and not really worth the number of times the dough forced the cover off and spilled over onto the heating coil. It's better simply to accept that this bread as baked in the electronic oven is going to emerge with a slightly rounded top. The squarish shape of the machine's pan will give you a close approximation of the real thing on the other five sides, and the flavor and texture will be right on target.

Make sure the butter called for in the recipe is either soft or sliced very thin before being added to the other ingredients, as otherwise it is apt not to be incorporated evenly in the batter. You may notice at the beginning of the mixing cycle that the dough seems far too dry and the machine seems to be simply stirring flour. Give it time, and it will churn together the well-kneaded dough for a good, rich sandwich loaf.

SMALL	LARGE
1/2 cup water	1 1/4 cups water
1/4 cup unsalted butter	1/2 cup unsalted butter
2 cups unbleached all-purpose flour	4 cups unbleached all-purpose flour
1 teaspoon sugar	2 teaspoons sugar
1/2 to 1 1/2 teaspoons salt to taste	1 to 2 teaspoons salt to taste
1 teaspoon active dry yeast	1 1/2 teaspoons active dry yeast

Pour the water into your bread machine baking pan and add the butter, remembering to slice it fairly thin if taking it cold from the refrigerator, as such a quantity dumped unceremoniously into the pan will fail to blend smoothly with the other ingredients. Measure in the flour, sugar, salt, and yeast, reserving the leavening to place in its separate dispenser if this feature is provided on your machine. If the directions that came with the model you have specify spooning the leavening into the pan at the start of operations, however, add the flour, sugar, and salt before the water and butter.

Bake the loaf on your machine's quick, or rapid-bake, cycle.

Beer Bread

Beer and bread have been intertwined in history ever since the Egyptians discovered zymurgy, whose listing in the dictionary I found as a child, much to my delight, to be the very last entry and a rare and challenging appendage in a game of Scrabble. Zymurgy, the art of fermentation, involves the harnessing of yeast to produce beer, bread, soy sauce, or any of a number of other less-familiar fermented products.

Egyptologists recently unearthed some apparently viable grains of wheat at the ancient Egyptian ruins of Tel el Amarna. They've planted a crop of this wheat and are planning to replicate the beer of the Pharaohs. "Whether there was one sourdough for bread and another for beer, we do not know," they observe. Outside of that comment, I've found no reference to the bread of the Pharaohs, the focus of the research seemingly being on the beer.

Considerable analysis is being devoted to the matter of regulating the temperature of the brew-to-be. "It gets pretty hot in Tel el Amarna, and excessive heat would destroy the enzymes needed to make sugar," the scientists reason. The ancient Egyptian zymologists' solution seems to have been to use special porous pottery for the fermentation process, enabling evaporation to cool the liquid as it rested.

There were no hops in ancient Egypt with which to flavor the Pharaohs' brew. Research seems to indicate that herbs, cinnamon, even dates, were used for this purpose.

Whatever the case, beer, albeit of the hopped variety, has long been used in Europe as the liquid of choice in many breads, to which it adds, besides keeping quality, a pleasantly rough texture and its own distinctive flavor. Dark beers like porter and stout contribute extra tang. It's a good idea to let the beer go flat before using it for bread. Otherwise the beating action of the kneading blade may cause the frothy dough to foam over.

SMALL

1 cup (⅔ of a 12-ounce can or bottle) flat beer

1 tablespoon canola or olive oil

2¼ cups unbleached all-purpose flour

2 tablespoons sugar

1½ teaspoons active dry yeast

LARGE

1½ cups (1 12-ounce can or bottle) flat beer

2 tablespoons canola or olive oil

3½ cups unbleached all-purpose flour

¼ cup sugar

2 teaspoons active dry yeast

If the instructions for the bread machine you have specify that the leavening is to be placed in the bottom of your baking pan first thing, add the flour and sugar before the beer and oil. Otherwise, pour the beer into the pan, followed by the canola or olive oil, then measure in the flour, sugar, and yeast. If your machine features a separate dispenser for leavening, spoon the yeast in there.

Use your machine's quick cycle for baking this bread.

Sesame Oatmeal Bread

The sesame in this loaf comes as a lovely surprise when one bites into it, especially when the seeds are toasted beforehand, although both that step and glazing the finished loaf with more of the decorative grains are optional. The tendency of oatmeal to weigh down a dough, resulting in a fairly compact bread, is compensated for in this recipe by the sour cream, which helps to give a loaf extra height.

SMALL	LARGE
1¼ cups sour cream or yogurt, regular or low-fat	1½ cups sour cream or yogurt, regular or low-fat
1 tablespoon unsalted butter or canola oil	2 tablespoons unsalted butter or canola oil
2 cups unbleached all-purpose flour	3 cups unbleached all-purpose flour
¾ cup uncooked oatmeal (not instant)	1¼ cups uncooked oatmeal (not instant)
1 tablespoon dark brown sugar	2 tablespoons dark brown sugar
¾ cup sesame seeds, toasted if desired	1¼ cups sesame seeds, toasted if desired
¼ to 1 teaspoon salt to taste	½ to 1½ teaspoons salt to taste
1½ teaspoons active dry yeast	2 teaspoons active dry yeast

Scoop the sour cream or yogurt into your baking machine bread pan and add the butter or canola oil, unless the instructions that came with your machine specify that the yeast is to be placed in the bottom of the pan first thing, followed by the other dry ingredients and then the liquids. Add the flour, oatmeal, brown sugar, sesame seeds, salt, and yeast, following the directions given for your particular machine in incorporating the yeast.

Bake the loaf on the machine's quick cycle.

Bulgarian Cheese Bread

There's a Bulgarian cheese called *sirene* that in its native country is often stuffed between layers of dough to make, when baked, a delicious cheese-filled triple-decker loaf traditionally served with tea. I've been unable to find *sirene* in the United States. But it's very similar to the Greek cheese feta, which is readily available.

A substitution more difficult to effect than that of replacing *sirene* with feta in a recipe is inducing a bread machine to bake the equivalent of a layered loaf. Short of using the device simply to mix and knead the dough and then shaping the loaf by hand and baking it in a conventional pan in a conventional oven — something which if I'm going to do I'll do without using the bread machine at all — there's no way of making this traditional *Tootmanik s gotovo testo* in the electronic oven. But the machine-made loaf that results from the recipe given here is a very tasty adaptation of the original bread, with a supremely silky crumb.

SMALL	LARGE
¾ cup buttermilk	1¼ cups buttermilk
1 teaspoon unsalted butter or olive oil	2 teaspoons unsalted butter or olive oil
1 teaspoon honey	2 teaspoons honey
6 ounces feta cheese	8 ounces feta cheese
2 cups unbleached all-purpose flour	3 cups unbleached all-purpose flour
½ to 1½ teaspoons salt to taste	1 to 2 teaspoons salt to taste
1½ teaspoons active dry yeast	2 teaspoons active dry yeast

Remember that if the instructions that came with your bread machine call for the yeast to be placed in the baking pan first, the flour and salt should be added before the liquids and the feta. Otherwise, pour the buttermilk into your pan and add the butter or olive oil, honey, feta cheese, flour, salt, and, if the instructions for your machine so direct, the yeast. If your machine has a separate dispenser for leavening, spoon the yeast into it after all the other ingredients have been measured into the baking pan.

Set the machine to its rapid-bake cycle for this loaf.

Basque Shepherd's Bread

This is a very light, open-textured, simple bread that is pleasant indeed fresh from the electronic bakery. It doesn't keep very well, but then, considering that the Basque shepherds of northern Spain from whom it derives its name would prepare the dough each morning for that evening's meal, one can well understand that keeping quality was not high on the list of necessary attributes for the bread.

The shepherd would place the dough in a covered iron pot and bury it in the coals of his Pyrenees campfire before setting out each day to tend his flock. On his return in the evening, a warm pot of bread would be waiting for him. Traditionally, the top of the bread was slashed to form a cross before the meal, and the first piece of each loaf was always given to the herder's trusty sheepdog.

The similarity in shape between the shepherd's ancient iron kettle and the modern pan one buries in the electronic campfire of one's bread machine suggested the suitability of this particular loaf for the automated home bakery.

SMALL
3/4 cup water
1 tablespoon olive oil
1 3/4 cups unbleached all-purpose
    flour

1 tablespoon sugar
1 teaspoon dried sage
1/2 to 1 teaspoon salt to taste
1 1/2 teaspoons active dry yeast

LARGE

1¼ cups water

2 tablespoons olive oil

3 cups unbleached all-purpose
   flour

4 teaspoons sugar

2 teaspoons dried sage

1 to 2 teaspoons salt to
   taste

2 teaspoons active dry yeast

Pour the water and olive oil into the baking pan of your bread machine and add the flour, sugar, sage, salt, and yeast, placing the leavening in its own separate dispenser if your machine has such. Remember, however, that if the instructions accompanying the model you have call for placing the leavening in the bottom of the pan first thing, then the other dry ingredients should be added next, before the water and oil.

Bake the loaf on your machine's quick cycle.

Stuffing Bread

This loaf started out to be homemade stuffing bread for chicken and turkey, the idea being to freeze it up so as to have it ready on short notice. The idea works fine in principle, but the bread is so fragrant that soon after its removal from the electronic oven, one is apt to find whole slices of it missing. All the same, even two half loaves rescued for their original purpose, safely diced and tucked away in the freezer before they too slip away under slabs of a sharp cheese or, yes, enveloping chicken salad, will do the average small bird nicely.

SMALL	LARGE
1 cup water or vegetable broth	1½ cups water or vegetable broth
2 teaspoons olive oil	1 tablespoon olive oil
1 teaspoon unsulphured molasses	2 teaspoons unsulphured molasses
2 cups unbleached all-purpose flour	3 cups unbleached all-purpose flour
½ cup uncooked oatmeal (not instant)	¾ cup uncooked oatmeal (not instant)
½ cup cornmeal	¾ cup cornmeal
2 tablespoons dehydrated parsley	3 tablespoons dehydrated parsley
1 tablespoon dehydrated minced onion	4 teaspoons dehydrated minced onion
1 teaspoon dried rosemary	1½ teaspoons dried rosemary
1 teaspoon dried sage	1½ teaspoons dried sage
½ teaspoon dried thyme	1 teaspoon dried thyme
½ teaspoon pepper	1 teaspoon pepper
¼ teaspoon garlic powder or 1 clove fresh garlic, pressed	½ teaspoon garlic powder or 2 cloves fresh garlic, pressed
½ to 1½ teaspoons salt to taste	1 to 2 teaspoons salt to taste
1½ teaspoons active dry yeast	2 teaspoons active dry yeast

Pour the water or vegetable broth into your bread machine baking pan and add the olive oil and molasses, unless the instructions that came with your machine call for placing the yeast in the bottom of the pan and reserving the liquids till last, adding them after the dry ingredients. Measure in the flour, oatmeal, cornmeal, parsley, onion, rosemary, sage, thyme, pepper, garlic, salt, and yeast. If your machine has a separate dispenser for leavening, spoon the yeast in there.

Use the rapid-bake setting on your machine for this loaf.

Faux French White Bread

European flour is softer than the bread flour found in the United States. In some ways it's more like our cake flour. I once tried to duplicate the texture by mixing some cake flour in with the bread flour I was using, hoping, among other things, to achieve in some miraculous random way the crisp crust crowning so many of the loaves and rolls I remembered from the Continent.

My experiment didn't work out as I'd hoped. The bread that emerged from my electronic oven was soft and tender inside and out. But it was a very nice, homely sort of bread, "a welcome change," as my wife, Susan, put it, "from a rich diet of the more colorful and heavily flavored breads." She likes slices of this loaf toasted for breakfast with butter and apricot jam. It's marvelous with a bitter orange marmalade as well.

You'll note that a bit of barley malt syrup is used in the recipe given here. Malt, available at health-food stores and by mail order, is extracted from sprouted barley. An enzyme in it called diastase produces the natural sugar maltose, which is what imparts the familiar malt flavoring to real, old-fashioned malted milk. Barley malt syrup is a viscous semiliquid that adds a warm flavor to what otherwise might be bland fare. Make sure you use plain barley malt syrup, not the hop-flavored malt sold for home beer brewing. Hop malt has a bitter taste.

SMALL	LARGE
1 cup sour cream or yogurt, regular or low-fat	*1½ cups sour cream or yogurt, regular or low-fat*
¼ cup water	*⅓ cup water*
1 tablespoon olive oil	*4 teaspoons olive oil*
1 tablespoon barley malt syrup	*1 tablespoon barley malt syrup*
1½ cups unbleached all-purpose flour	*2½ cups unbleached all-purpose flour*
1 cup cake flour	*1½ cups cake flour*
¼ cup whole-wheat flour	*½ cup whole-wheat flour*
½ to 1½ teaspoons salt to taste	*1 to 2 teaspoons salt to taste*
1½ teaspoons active dry yeast	*2 teaspoons active dry yeast*

Scoop the sour cream or yogurt into the baking pan of your bread machine and add the water, olive oil, and barley malt syrup, unless the instructions for your machine specify that the yeast is to be placed in the bottom of the pan first thing, in which case these liquid ingredients should be added last, after all the dry ingredients. Measure in the all-purpose, cake, and whole-wheat flours, the salt, and the yeast, placing the leavening in its own separate dispenser if your machine has one.

To bake the loaf, set your machine to its rapid cycle.

4 · Breads from the Garden

THERE'S NO RECIPE in this chapter for zucchini bread, even though it's one of the most popular of all garden breads. I'm zucchinied out. I haven't even planted any in the garden this year, a rash move I may regret as the summer moves along. Then again, my neighbors have a few plants, and in a good year a few zucchini plants have been known to produce enough zucchini to supply the whole village.

Besides, one zucchini bread recipe is really enough, and I furnished that in my first book of breads, *The Bread Machine Bakery Book*. I also incorporated there a recipe for carrot bread, that other ever-popular bread from the garden, so that's done. But since there's no end to the vegetables that can be used to enrich and flavor breads, there are always more recipes to be tried. And their usefulness doesn't end with the growing season, for today's modern supermarket provides a "garden" year-round. Many dried or frozen vegetables make admirable additions to a winter's loaf as well.

Vegetable breads tend to be richer and more filling than their plainer counterparts. So they are more often found in the company of one-pot meals like stews and soups — another reason why they make wonderful winter breads — than at the side of a full-course meal.

Italian Potato Bread

Pasta, of course! Risotto, even. But potatoes — do they even have potatoes in Italy? That was the question I couldn't help asking myself when I first heard about Italian potato bread. Somehow I'd always thought of potatoes as a staple more or less exclusive to northern Europe.

I've since learned that they grow some very nice potatoes in Italy, and they use them in bread much as the Hungarians do. But they don't put any caraway in their loaves, and the bread contains a minimal amount of liquid. You'll find no water in this recipe beyond that contained in the boiled potatoes themselves. A little olive oil provides the only additional moisture.

Because of the dryness of the ingredients, the dough starts out crumbly, looking as if it will never hold together. Eventually, however, moisture is squeezed from the potatoes and the dough begins to resemble a stiff biscuit batter. It makes a delicious loaf, "so tender," Susan remarked, "that the only thing holding it together is the crust."

Boil the potatoes, if you don't happen to have some left over in the refrigerator, and roughly mash enough of them to fill your measuring cup. Regular Maine boiling potatoes work best. If you use the drier Idaho baking potatoes, you may need to add a couple of tablespoonfuls of water from the pot in which they were boiled to help soften the dough. Check the bread pan in your machine after the first ten minutes or so of mixing to see how the dough is forming. If it is really dry and crumbly, add a little potato water to soften it.

SMALL	LARGE
1 cup mashed potatoes	*2 cups mashed potatoes*
2 tablespoons olive oil	*¼ cup olive oil*
1½ cups unbleached all-purpose flour	*2 cups unbleached all-purpose flour*
½ to 1 teaspoon salt to taste	*1 to 2 teaspoons salt to taste*
1½ teaspoons active dry yeast	*2 teaspoons active dry yeast*

If the instructions for your machine call for the yeast to be placed in the bottom of the baking pan, the flour and salt should be added before the potatoes and olive oil. Otherwise, scoop the mashed potatoes into your bread machine pan and add the olive oil, then the flour, salt, and yeast. If the machine you have features a separate yeast dispenser for leavening, add the yeast there.

The rapid-bake setting on your machine is the one to use for this loaf.

Savory Cheese-Tomato Bread

Yuppie bread, the kids call it. And I guess that now somewhat disparaging adjective befits this bread. On the other hand, sun-dried tomatoes and sharp Italian cheeses were around for centuries before their eighties' new debut in the media style pages. Certainly they are a great combination.

This bread is for hearty winter stews and hot soups. It's also good with cheese, naturally, or simply drizzled with olive oil.

SMALL	LARGE
½ cup heavy cream	¾ cup heavy cream
2 tablespoons olive oil	3 tablespoons olive oil
2 eggs	3 eggs
½ cup sun-dried tomato slices, reconstituted according to the package instructions	¾ cup sun-dried tomato slices, reconstituted according to the package instructions
¼ cup chopped scallions	½ cup chopped scallions
2 large cloves garlic, crushed	3 large cloves garlic, crushed
¾ cup grated sharp Italian cheese such as Parmesan, Romano, or Asiago	1 cup grated sharp Italian cheese such as Parmesan, Romano, or Asiago
2 cups unbleached all-purpose flour	3½ cups unbleached all-purpose flour
½ to 1½ teaspoons salt to taste	1 to 2 teaspoons salt to taste
1½ teaspoons active dry yeast	2 teaspoons active dry yeast

Pour the cream and olive oil into your bread pan, unless the instructions for your machine direct you to place the yeast in the bottom of the pan first thing, in which case the other dry ingredients should be added next, the liquids last. Break in the eggs and add the tomato slices, scallions, garlic, grated cheese, flour, and salt. Measure the yeast into its own dispenser if your machine has one. If not, scatter it over the other dry ingredients.

Bake the loaf on your machine's quick cycle.

Tex-Mex Corn Bread

This bread is Mexican more in imagination than in reality. One evening as I was making our family's version of cheese quesadillas, stuffed to overflowing with Monterey Jack, peeled whole green chilies, and sour cream and slathered extravagantly with piquant tomato sauce, we found ourselves with unexpected company when one of Revell's friends stayed for dinner. To stretch the meal, I flicked the bread machine to its quick cycle and concocted what I hoped would be a suitable corn bread.

The dinner being a spicy south-of-the-border one, corn seemed a natural ingredient for the loaf. So did the red peppers, whose pieces one bites into unexpectedly. Don't ask me how the wheat germ crept into the recipe, that particular ingredient being more regional to Bemidji, Minnesota, than Baja California. The yeast, used instead of the baking powder commonly associated with corn breads in this country, contributes to the smoothness of the loaf.

If you peek into your bread machine early in the mixing of this bread, you'll note that the dough seems too dry. Leave it alone. Once the kneading process has been completed, the moisture squeezed from the corn kernels will have added enough liquid to make a smooth, silky, stiff dough. The final loaf is substantial, with a very even, moist crumb.

Because the bread was an afterthought to the original menu, even though we delayed dinner for half an hour we ended up trying to slice the loaf hot from the pan, which meant that it crumbled. Really hot bread does not slice well. Not only does the crust crumble, but the center of the loaf tends to compact and become sticky. Better to break the bread into chunks in such circumstances. Besides, there's something pleasingly primitive about tearing off a hunk of steaming fresh bread. Also chunks are twice as efficient as slices at mopping up extra sauce.

SMALL	LARGE
1 11-ounce can of corn with liquid	*1 16-ounce can of corn with liquid*
1 tablespoon unsalted butter or canola oil	*2 tablespoons unsalted butter or canola oil*
1 tablespoon unsulphured molasses	*2 tablespoons unsulphured molasses*
2 cups unbleached all-purpose flour	*3½ cups unbleached all-purpose flour*
⅓ cup wheat germ	*½ cup wheat germ*
1½ teaspoons crushed red peppers	*2 teaspoons crushed red peppers*
½ teaspoon coriander	*1 teaspoon coriander*
¼ to 1 teaspoon salt to taste	*½ to 1½ teaspoons salt to taste*
1½ teaspoons active dry yeast	*2 teaspoons active dry yeast*

Pour the corn with its liquid into your bread machine baking pan and add the butter or canola oil and the molasses. Then measure in the flour, wheat germ, crushed red peppers, coriander, and salt. Place the yeast in its own separate dispenser if your machine has one. If it doesn't, scatter the leavening over the other dry ingredients. However, if the instructions for the model you have specify placing the leavening in the pan first thing, add the other dry ingredients next and end with the liquids.

Set your machine to its rapid-bake cycle for this loaf.

Spinach Bread

Although the kids disparagingly call it "Popeye bread," this unusual marbled loaf is a tasty, quickly and easily made conversation starter for any adult gathering. Using your electronic oven's delayed baking mode, it is even possible simply to unwrap a package of frozen spinach and plop the verdant ice block right into the pan along with the rest of the ingredients. But in that case allow plenty of time, four to six hours, for defrosting. You want the spinach to be soft before the batter is mixed. If the greens are still frozen when the machine's agitator starts its job, the nonstick finish on your bread pan may become scratched.

This method doesn't work with machines requiring you to put the yeast in the bottom of the pan with the other ingredients on top of it. The spinach water will filter down to the leavening as it slowly thaws, activating it too soon.

Whether you use the spinach frozen, thawed, or zapped by your microwave, the liquid from the package is the only moisture provided for the bread. So if you plan to defrost the spinach beforehand, make sure you reserve all the liquid to add to the pan with the greens themselves.

For a slightly milder, sweeter loaf, brown the garlic called for in an extra tablespoonful of olive oil before adding it to the other ingredients.

SMALL

*1 10-ounce package frozen spinach,
thawed, with liquid*

1 tablespoon olive oil

*1 clove garlic, minced, and browned
if desired in 1 tablespoon olive
oil*

2 cups unbleached all-purpose flour

1/2 teaspoon sugar

1/4 teaspoon grated nutmeg

1/2 to 1 teaspoon salt to taste

1 1/2 teaspoons active dry yeast

LARGE

*2 10-ounce packages frozen
spinach, thawed, with liquid*

2 tablespoons olive oil

*2 cloves garlic, minced, and
browned if desired in 1
tablespoon olive oil*

4 cups unbleached all-purpose flour

1 teaspoon sugar

1/2 teaspoon grated nutmeg

1 to 2 teaspoons salt to taste

2 teaspoons active dry yeast

Place the spinach with its water in your baking pan, spoon in the olive oil, and add the garlic, flour, sugar, nutmeg, salt, and yeast, following the directions that came with your machine for incorporating the leavening.

Bake the loaf on your machine's quick cycle. If the spinach was placed in the pan frozen and you are using the delayed-baking mode, remember to allow four to six hours for defrosting when setting the timer.

Light Onion Bread

Onion breads in this country tend to be dark. An exception is the bialy, the roll originally from the town of Bialystok in Poland. But throughout the low countries of Europe, light onion loaves, combining the once supposed social refinement of white flour with the zest of an oniony peasant bread, are very popular.

The bread presented here retains its light color while incorporating a bit of rye for added flavor. It goes particularly well with sweet butter and a hearty garden-fresh vegetable soup. Start the potatoes for the soup early, and you can borrow a little of the potato water for the bread.

SMALL

1 cup plain or potato water

2 teaspoons canola oil

1 egg

2 cups unbleached all-purpose flour

1 cup rye flour

1 to 2 tablespoons dehydrated
   minced onion to taste

1/2 to 1 1/2 teaspoons salt to taste

1 1/2 teaspoons active dry yeast

LARGE

1 1/2 cups plain or potato water

1 tablespoon canola oil

2 eggs

3 cups unbleached all-purpose flour

1 1/2 cups rye flour

2 to 4 tablespoons dehydrated
   minced onion to taste

1 to 2 teaspoons salt to taste

2 teaspoons active dry yeast

Unless directed by the instructions for the particular bread machine you have to reserve the liquids and moist ingredients for your bread dough till last, pour the water into your baking pan and add the canola oil, egg or eggs, all-purpose and rye flours, onion, and salt. Add the yeast as directed for your machine.

The rapid-bake cycle on your electronic oven is the best one for this bread.

Olive Bread

I was putting a loaf of this silky-textured bread on the cooling rack when Revell, covered waist-down with mud from frog catching, wandered into the kitchen.

"And what's this one, Dad?" His tone was suspicious. The day before, I'd been working on a caper loaf — the recipe for which, probably to everyone's relief, is not included in this volume — and he now approached the tasting of each new bread with a certain reservation.

"Never mind," I replied, using a phrase I have repeatedly admonished the kids not to use.

"Come on!"

"Well, it's an olive loaf."

"You're pushing it, Dad, you're really pushing it."

Perhaps, from his perspective, that was so. The flavor of olives in this bread is subtle but definitely present, and olives seem to be an acquired taste. All the same, olive bread is a lovely foil for thinly sliced sharp Italian cheeses.

Speaking of cheese, the cream cheese — what else with olives? — in the recipe provides some of the required moisture. Cut it into small chunks for less laborious blending when the machine is kneading the dough.

SMALL

¼ cup water or olive liquid
reserved from draining the olives
1 tablespoon olive oil
1 tablespoon honey
1 egg
2 ounces cream cheese, chunked

½ cup drained green pimento-
stuffed olives
2 cups unbleached all-purpose
flour
½ to 1½ teaspoons salt to taste
1½ teaspoons active dry yeast

LARGE

1/3 cup water or olive liquid
reserved from draining the
olives
1 tablespoon olive oil
2 tablespoons honey
2 eggs

4 ounces cream cheese, chunked
1 cup drained green pimento-
stuffed olives
3 cups unbleached all-purpose
flour
1 to 2 teaspoons salt to taste
2 teaspoons active dry yeast

Unless the instructions that came with your machine call for placing the yeast in the very bottom of the pan, followed by the other dry
ingredients and then the liquids, pour the water or reserved olive
liquid into your baking pan and add the olive oil, honey, egg or eggs,
cream cheese, and olives. Measure in the flour, salt, and yeast, reserving the last for its own separate dispenser if your machine has
one.

Use the machine's rapid-bake cycle for this loaf.

Rosemary Bread

Mediterranean country cooking is often redolent with the pun-
gent, earthy scent of rosemary. The herb goes well with many
hearty foods, from roast pork and lamb to robustly flavored seafood
such as bluefish. But it's also an excellent flavoring in more delicate
cuisine. The light bread to which it adds its subtle seasoning here
complements chowders and rich vegetable soups wonderfully. I'm
always reminded of the area around Camargue in southern France
when the fragrant, sunny loaf emerges from its pan.

You'll notice a liberal quantity of olive oil in the recipe for this
bread. If you can lay your hands on a flask of the dark, extra-virgin
cold-pressed variety, by all means use it for the additional flavor and
color it will contribute.

SMALL	LARGE
½ cup milk, whole or skim	*⅔ cup milk, whole or skim*
¼ cup water or vegetable broth	*⅓ cup water or vegetable broth*
¼ cup olive oil	*⅓ cup olive oil*
2 cups unbleached all-purpose flour	*3 cups unbleached all-purpose flour*
1 tablespoon dried or 3 tablespoons fresh rosemary	*2 tablespoons dried or ⅓ cup fresh rosemary*
¼ teaspoon dried sage	*½ teaspoon dried sage*
½ to 1½ teaspoons salt to taste	*1 to 2 teaspoons salt to taste*
1½ teaspoons active dry yeast	*2 teaspoons active dry yeast*

Pour the milk, water or vegetable broth, and olive oil into your bread machine baking pan, unless the instructions for your machine direct you to put the yeast into the pan first, followed by the other dry ingredients and then the liquids. Add the flour, rosemary, sage, salt, and yeast, placing the leavening in its own separate dispenser if your machine has one.

Bake the loaf on your machine's quick cycle.

5 · Breads from the Orchard

A LOAF OF BREAD, a jug of wine, and thou" — the words were surely penned advisedly. Whether as wine or juice, the sweet, smooth quality of fruit in its liquid form complements the fibrous texture of grains. Then too, the natural sugars in fruit aid yeast in leavening bread.

I particularly like to step out to the old orchard in what is now our back pasture to gather apples on a summer morn. The horses have stripped the bark off half the trees, and insects seem to have scavenged the other half. The fruit is scabby and not particularly attractive — it's impossible to grow picture-perfect apples anymore without massive spraying — but oh, what flavor! I bring the apples into the kitchen, Susan makes a wonderful pink applesauce, and I slip the ingredients for a batch of spiced apple granola bread into the electronic oven before the heat of the day sets in.

With the variety of fresh produce available just about everywhere these days, one needn't have an orchard of one's own in order to harvest the benefits of newly plucked fruit. For that matter, dried fruits make wonderful winter breads, traditional cold-weather pick-me-ups rich in vitamins and flavor.

Spiced Apple Granola Bread

Here's a healthy loaf that from a cursory glance at the recipe might seem to have just too many things in it. All too often as the ingredients in a recipe increase in number, the taste and texture of the finished result abate. This bread is a notable exception. Everything from the granola and the sour cream to the honey and fragrant cinnamon enhances its flavor. Molly, a school friend of Tanya's staying with us at the time when the baking for this book was in full swing and inundated with bread along with the rest of the family, rated it one of her favorite loaves.

The dough starts out quite stiff, and it's a good idea to peek into the bread pan about five to ten minutes into the initial mixing cycle to see if the sides need scraping down with a rubber spatula, particularly if you are baking the large loaf.

The granola I generally use happens to be the Erewhon version of the cereal, but other brands work well too.

SMALL	LARGE
1 cup sour cream or yogurt, regular or low-fat	1½ cups sour cream or yogurt, regular or low-fat
1 tablespoon unsalted butter or canola oil	2 tablespoons unsalted butter or canola oil
½ cup honey	⅔ cup honey
1 egg	1 egg
1 unpeeled apple, diced	1½ unpeeled apples, diced
1 cup granola	2 cups granola
1½ cups unbleached all-purpose flour	2½ cups unbleached all-purpose flour
½ cup whole-wheat flour	½ cup whole-wheat flour
1 teaspoon cinnamon	1½ teaspoons cinnamon
½ teaspoon grated nutmeg	1 teaspoon grated nutmeg
¼ to 1 teaspoon salt to taste	½ to 2 teaspoons salt to taste
1½ teaspoons active dry yeast	2 teaspoons active dry yeast

Scoop the sour cream or yogurt into your baking pan along with the butter or canola oil, honey, and egg. Add the apple, granola, all-purpose and whole-wheat flours, cinnamon, nutmeg, and salt. Place the yeast in its own dispenser if your machine has one; otherwise scatter it over the rest of the ingredients. If it is to be placed in the bottom of the pan first thing instead, don't forget to reverse the order in which you add the liquid and the dry ingredients.

Bake the bread on your machine's quick cycle.

Citrus Cherry Bread

Citrus oils allow you to add most of the flavor of freshly grated lemon, lime, or orange peel without the knuckles. Personally, I still prefer my zest fresh from the fruit most of the time. But if I'm out of the fruit or baking in a hurry, particularly with a bread machine, being able to reach for a bottle of orange or lemon oil is a real convenience.

Dried cherries are another item I try to keep on the shelf. They don't always remain there unless hidden behind jars of capers or cans of olives, commodities to which the kids haven't yet taken the same gourmet shine they've taken to the cherries, but I do try.

My favorite among the dried cherries is the Montmorency, sweet yet tangy, and ever so munchable. As Revell remarked, picking the red bits out of a slice of bread before eating the bread itself, "These cherries are great!" I'd agree, adding only that the bread is too.

SMALL

½ cup sour cream
¼ cup unsalted butter or canola oil
1 egg
½ teaspoon orange or lemon oil
¾ cup dried cherries
2 cups unbleached all-purpose flour
⅓ cup firmly packed dark brown sugar
½ to 1½ teaspoons salt to taste
1½ teaspoons active dry yeast

LARGE

3/4 cup sour cream

1/3 cup unsalted butter or canola oil

2 eggs

1 teaspoon orange or lemon oil

1 1/4 cups dried cherries

3 1/2 cups unbleached all-purpose flour

1/2 cup firmly packed dark brown sugar

1 to 2 teaspoons salt to taste

2 teaspoons active dry yeast

Scoop the sour cream into your bread machine pan and add the butter or canola oil, unless the directions for the model you have instruct you to place the leavening in the very bottom of the pan first, the other dry ingredients next, and the liquids last. If you are using butter straight from the refrigerator, it will be cold and hard, so, because you are using a sizable quantity, it should be cut into chunks before being placed in the pan, as otherwise it will fail to blend into the dough evenly. Break the egg or eggs into the pan and add the orange or lemon oil, cherries, flour, brown sugar, salt, and yeast, placing the yeast in its own separate dispenser if your machine has such.

Set the machine to its rapid-bake cycle for this loaf.

Apricot Bread

Apricots bring to mind, for me, scenes from the movie version of *Lost Horizons*, set somewhere in Hunza land, where eternal youth springs from this stone fruit in alliance with lots of yogurt. They also recall my grandmother's homemade *marillenbrand*, an apricot brandy that, while it might not extend life, certainly made it seem eternal.

Today, fresh apricots have more or less vanished from my experience. Oh, I know they can be bought in supermarkets, but the hard, dry, tart spheroids found there have very little in common with the sun-warmed taste bursts I remember picking ripe from the trees, always checking first for yellow jackets, which loved them as much as I did.

Surprisingly, the dried apricots likewise available in supermarkets still make a great nibble, and also a good sweet bread that adds a sumptuous touch to an afternoon tea, not to mention a nutritious boost to a child's after-school snack. For an even more tempting loaf, give it an apricot jam glaze such as the one found among the recipes in the chapter "Topping It All Off."

SMALL	LARGE
1 cup milk, whole or skim	*1½ cups milk, whole or skim*
1 tablespoon walnut oil	*2 tablespoons walnut oil*
2 tablespoons unsulphured molasses	*3 tablespoons unsulphured molasses*
1 cup dried apricots, halved	*1½ cups dried apricots, halved*
2 cups unbleached all-purpose flour	*3¼ cups unbleached all-purpose flour*
1 cup unprocessed wheat bran	*¾ cup unprocessed wheat bran*
¼ to 1 teaspoon salt to taste	*½ to 1½ teaspoons salt to taste*
1½ teaspoons active dry yeast	*2 teaspoons active dry yeast*

Place the milk, walnut oil, and molasses in your machine's bread pan, add the apricots, and measure in the flour, wheat bran, and salt. Last, unless the instructions that came with your machine call for reversing the order in which the leavening and the liquids are incorporated, spoon in the yeast, using the separate dispenser for it if your machine has one.

Bake the loaf on your machine's quick cycle.

Three Nuts Apricot Bread

Nuts and apricots seem somehow to have a natural affinity for each other. Certainly in this loaf, Susan's favorite for cream cheese sandwiches, they are a magnificent combination.

Following personal preference, I make this bread with an assortment of the tree nuts such as almonds, hazelnuts, pecans, and walnuts. But groundnut fans can successfully substitute peanuts, reducing the salt in the recipe if the nuts are salted, for any or all of the nuts listed, cupful for cupful.

It's simplest to add the nuts whole and the apricots in the halves in which they usually come dried. Besides, with this method one bites into good-sized chunks of the rich nuts and fruit hidden in unexpected corners of the loaf. But if you prefer a more uniform loaf with fewer surprises, quarter the apricots and use chopped nuts.

SMALL
1 cup milk, whole or skim
1 tablespoon unsalted butter or walnut oil
1 tablespoon honey
1 egg
½ cup dried apricots, quartered if desired
½ cup blanched almonds, whole or chopped, or ½ to 1½ cups peanuts, replacing some or all of the other nuts listed
½ cup pecan halves or pieces
½ cup walnut halves or pieces or whole or chopped hazelnuts
1¾ cups unbleached all-purpose flour
¾ cup unprocessed wheat bran
½ to 1 teaspoon salt to taste
1½ teaspoons active dry yeast

LARGE
1½ cups milk, whole or skim
2 tablespoons unsalted butter or walnut oil
2 tablespoons honey
1 egg
1 cup dried apricots, quartered if desired
¾ cup blanched almonds, whole or chopped, or ¾ to 2¼ cups peanuts, replacing some or all of the other nuts listed
¾ cup pecan halves or pieces
¾ cup walnut halves or pieces or whole or chopped hazelnuts

2³/₄ cups unbleached all-purpose
  flour
1 cup unprocessed wheat bran

1 to 2 teaspoons salt to taste
2 teaspoons active dry yeast

Unless the instructions for your machine specify putting the yeast into the baking machine bread pan first thing and covering it with the other dry ingredients before adding the liquids, pour the milk into your pan, add the butter or walnut oil and the honey, and break the egg into the pan. Toss in the apricots, almonds or peanuts, and the pecans and walnuts or hazelnuts if you are using those in your mix. Then measure in the flour, wheat bran, salt, and yeast. If your machine has a separate dispenser for the leavening, place the yeast there.

The rapid-bake cycle on your machine is the best setting for this bread.

Plum Pecan Bread

Toward the end of the summer, small dark purple Italian prune plums make their way to market. To my mind these are really the best of baking plums, being juicy yet firm, and they go particularly well with nuts like pecans. But any ripe plums can be used in making this bread.

The flavorsome loaf is very tender, even when cooled. So it will need to be sliced thick, country fashion.

SMALL
³/₄ cup unsweetened prune juice
¹/₄ cup unsalted butter or canola oil
1 egg
1 cup chopped pitted plums
¹/₂ cup pecan halves

2¹/₂ cups unbleached all-purpose
  flour
¹/₂ to 1¹/₂ teaspoons salt to taste
1¹/₂ teaspoons active dry yeast

LARGE

⅞ cup unsweetened prune juice

5 tablespoons unsalted butter or
   canola oil

1 egg

⅔ cup chopped pitted plums

¾ cup pecan halves

4 cups unbleached all-
   purpose flour

1 to 2 teaspoons salt to taste

2 teaspoons active dry yeast

Pour the prune juice into your baking machine bread pan and add the butter, cut into small pieces for better blending if taken cold from the refrigerator, or canola oil if preferred. Break in the egg and add the plums, pecans, flour, salt, and yeast, positioning the yeast as directed for your particular machine. If the instructions that came with the model you have call for starting with the yeast, the other dry ingredients should be added before the liquid and moist ones.

To bake the loaf, use your machine's quick cycle.

Prune Bread

Prunes have bad press in the United States, relegated as they are largely to plain stewed compotes served the elderly for a number of health reasons. But in the Old World prunes are much esteemed, featuring in such gustatory delights as lekvar, the delicate plum butter of Central Europe, and slivovitz, the fiery brandy distilled around the Adriatic — and, in days gone by, in my grandmother's Viennese kitchen.

Here's a solid dark bread that makes a substantial breakfast for those who have only a slice of toast and coffee as their morning meal. Try it with cream cheese for extra sustenance and smoothness.

Be sure your machine is set to its quick cycle when you bake this bread. The regular, or long, cycle is apt to produce a bread the color of the prunes themselves.

SMALL

1 cup milk, whole or skim

*2 tablespoons unsalted butter or
  canola oil*

2 tablespoons lemon juice

1 cup pitted whole dry prunes

1 cup unbleached all-purpose flour

1 cup semolina flour

*½ cup uncooked oatmeal (not
  instant)*

½ teaspoon ground cloves

½ to 1½ teaspoons salt to taste

1½ teaspoons active dry yeast

LARGE

1½ cups milk, whole or skim

¼ cup unsalted butter or canola oil

¼ cup lemon juice

2 cups pitted whole dry prunes

*1¾ cups unbleached all-purpose
  flour*

1½ cups semolina flour

*1 cup uncooked oatmeal (not
  instant)*

1 teaspoon ground cloves

1 to 2 teaspoons salt to taste

2 teaspoons active dry yeast

Pour the milk into your baking pan and add the butter or canola oil, unless the directions for your machine instruct you to start with the yeast, followed by the dry and then the liquid ingredients. If you are making the large loaf and using butter straight from the refrigerator, cut it into chunks before placing it in the pan, so it will blend more easily with the other ingredients. Add the lemon juice, prunes, all-purpose and semolina flours, oatmeal, cloves, and salt. Then measure the yeast into its own dispenser if your machine has a separate container for leavening; otherwise, scatter it over the rest of the ingredients.

Use the machine's quick cycle for baking this bread.

6 · Crusty Concoctions

A CRUST OF BREAD" is one of those ambivalent expressions that can convey meanings ranging from derogatory to scrumptious. Then there's the "upper crust," whose reference to the highest ranks of society derives not from its physical position in a loaf of bread but from the fact that it used to be the portion placed before the most honored guest at a table. On the other hand, a "crusty" character has been an ill-tempered one ever since Achilles in Shakespeare's *Troilus and Cressida* called out to Thersites, "Thou crusty batch of nature, what's the news?"

As connotations differ, so do tastes. Myself, I love a good crust, either chewy or crisp. The *eckhaus,* or "corner house," as it's known in German, is my favorite part of a loaf, and I can think of no finer meal than a generous crust of pumpernickel or a fresh baguette spread with sweet butter and served with cheese. Revell, on the other hand, prefers the soft center slices with the least crust. The crusts he saves for fishing.

The breads represented in this section are flavorful delights, but they are particularly so for those who like a good crust. Note that I specified a good crust, not a great crust. The fact is that nothing yet devised has succeeded in duplicating the conditions of the stone hearth for baking bread, and no electronic bakery yet produced for the home can yield the huge free-form loaves of crusty white Italian bread or dark Bavarian pumpernickel found where the baker plies his trade and shapes his dough by hand. Then again, no stone hearth and no manual labor can produce good basic bread at the mere press of a button.

Country Bran Bread

H ere's a rough-hewn country loaf chock-full of bran and right up
to the latest health-food standards. Truth to tell, the bran phase
of our family's diet consciousness was relatively short-lived. After all,
one can eat only so many bran muffins, and much else presumably
enriched by the light brown flakes loses rather than gains in flavor.
During the height of the bran fad, I actually saw an ad for oat-bran
and honey ice cream. . . .

But this simple recipe puts bran to both healthy and enjoyable
use. Not sweet like bran muffins, the bread has a wonderful crust
outside, a soft, silky texture inside. The flavor is hearty, nutty, and so
pleasant that one would never suspect the loaf of being as highly
nutritious as it in fact is. It makes splendid toast and, in the summertime, abetted by sun-warmed tomatoes fresh from the garden, wickedly wonderful BLTs.

SMALL

1 cup water or vegetable broth
2 tablespoons olive oil
2 cups unbleached all-purpose flour
1 1/4 cup unprocessed wheat bran
1/2 to 1 1/2 teaspoons salt to taste
1 teaspoon active dry yeast

LARGE

1 1/2 cups water or vegetable broth
3 tablespoons olive oil
3 cups unbleached all-purpose flour
1 1/2 cups unprocessed wheat bran
1 to 2 teaspoons salt to taste
1 1/2 teaspoons active dry yeast

Remember that if the instructions accompanying your bread machine call for the yeast to be placed in the baking pan first, the
flour, bran, and salt should be added before the water or broth and
the oil. Otherwise, pour the water or vegetable broth into your
pan, spoon in the olive oil, then add the flour, bran, salt, and yeast,
reserving the leavening for its own separate dispenser if your machine has one.

Set the machine to its quick cycle to bake this loaf.

Flaky Bread

While whole-grain breads, acclaimed for their nutrition and roughage, have become staples in the kitchens of the health-conscious, not everyone likes chewy and/or crunchy kernels in his or her bread. However, flakes like those of the familiar oatmeal and the lesser-known wheat, barley, and rye available at health-food stores provide a commendable enough amount of roughage and nutrition per slice of the bread they enrich without as much chew as the whole-grain loaves present. The flakes also add a nubby interest to the crust, "the best part of this loaf," according to Susan. Brush the loaf with a simple egg glaze (a recipe for which is in the chapter "Topping It All Off") after baking and scatter some extra barley flakes over it for a crowning touch.

SMALL

¾ cup milk, whole or skim

1 tablespoon canola oil

1 tablespoon honey

1 egg

1¾ cups unbleached all-purpose flour

½ cup barley flakes

½ cup rye flakes

½ to 1½ teaspoons salt to taste

1½ teaspoons active dry yeast

LARGE

1¾ cups milk, whole or skim

2 tablespoons canola oil

2 tablespoons honey

1 egg

3 cups unbleached all-purpose flour

1 cup barley flakes

1 cup rye flakes

1 to 2 teaspoons salt to taste

2 teaspoons active dry yeast

Pour the milk into your baking machine pan and spoon in the canola oil and honey. Break the egg into the pan and add the flour along with the barley and rye flakes; then measure in the salt and yeast, placing the leavening in its own dispenser if your machine is equipped with such. If the directions for your machine specify that the yeast is to be placed in the bottom of the pan, remember to reverse the order in which you incorporate the liquid and the dry ingredients.

This loaf is best baked on your machine's quick cycle.

Whole-Wheat Crunch Bread

Here's a delightful loaf literally bursting with flavor. Millet is underutilized in our cuisine, and even when a recipe does call for it, it's usually in the form of flour. Here, the tiny seeds are used whole. Firm and crisp, unlike the more chewy wheat and other grains often incorporated unmilled in breads, they surprise one with their lilliputian nuggets of taste scattered throughout the loaf.

SMALL

1 cup sour cream or yogurt, regular or low-fat

2 tablespoons unsalted butter or canola oil

1 cup whole-wheat flour

3/4 cup unbleached all-purpose flour

1/2 cup millet seed

1/2 to 1 1/2 teaspoons salt to taste

1 1/2 teaspoons active dry yeast

LARGE

1 3/4 cups sour cream or yogurt, regular or low-fat

1/4 cup unsalted butter or canola oil

1 1/4 cups whole-wheat flour

1 1/4 cups unbleached all-purpose flour

3/4 cup millet seed

1 to 2 teaspoons salt to taste

2 teaspoons active dry yeast

Scoop the sour cream or yogurt into your bread machine baking pan and add the butter or canola oil. If you are making the large loaf and have opted for the butter in preference to the oil, cut it into chunks if taking it cold from the refrigerator, for easier blending. Measure the whole-wheat and all-purpose flours into the pan, then add the millet, salt, and yeast. For placement of the yeast, follow the directions provided with the particular bread machine model you have.

Bake the loaf on your machine's quick cycle.

Buckwheat Bread

B uckwheat, a relative, actually, of rhubarb, is one of those regional specialties like hominy grits. Most of the buckwheat produced in this country is grown in New England and upstate New York, and most of the flour is consumed in the form of buckwheat pancakes. In Europe, buckwheat in the form of kasha is a popular substitute for potatoes or rice, and in Japan, noodles called *soba* are made from it. The distinctive, earthy flour seems to be gaining renewed approbation in culinary circles, and here's a recipe for a handsome flat-topped loaf made with it that can only further its prestige.

SMALL	LARGE
½ cup plus 1 tablespoon water	*1 cup water*
2 teaspoons canola oil	*1 tablespoon canola oil*
2 teaspoons unsulphured molasses	*1 tablespoon unsulphured molasses*
1 egg	*1 egg*
2 cups unbleached all-purpose flour	*3 cups unbleached all-purpose flour*
¼ cup buckwheat flour	*½ cup buckwheat flour*
½ to 1 teaspoon salt to taste	*1 to 2 teaspoons salt to taste*
1½ teaspoons active dry yeast	*2 teaspoons active dry yeast*

Pour the water into your bread machine baking pan, unless the directions that came with the model you have instruct that you place the leavening in the pan first, in which case the other dry ingredients should be added before the liquids. Measure in the canola oil and molasses and break the egg into the pan. Add the all-purpose and buckwheat flours, the salt, and the yeast, placing the leavening in its own dispenser if a separate container is provided for it on your machine.

Set the machine on either its quick or its regular cycle to bake this loaf.

Barley Bread

Barley breads are celebrated for their moistness and denseness. However, even when fully baked, the loaves often remain slightly sticky, with a vaguely undercooked feel to them. Here's a recipe that avoids that problem, because the millet flour somehow absorbs the stickiness.

Like most barley bread recipes, this one calls for a considerable proportion of regular flour. Barley flour alone will give you a loaf whose heft is reminiscent of the Mesopotamian building bricks found in the region where the grain was first cultivated.

This bread is firm and sweet, with a golden crust. It makes superb dry toast.

SMALL	LARGE
¾ cup water or vegetable broth	*1½ cups water or vegetable broth*
1 tablespoon canola oil	*4 teaspoons canola oil*
1 egg	*2 eggs*
1½ cups unbleached all-purpose flour	*3 cups unbleached all-purpose flour*
¾ cup barley flour	*1¼ cups barley flour*
¼ cup millet flour	*½ cup millet flour*
1 tablespoon dark brown sugar	*2 tablespoons dark brown sugar*
½ to 1½ teaspoons salt to taste	*1 to 2 teaspoons salt to taste*
1½ teaspoons active dry yeast	*2 teaspoons active dry yeast*

Unless directed by the instructions for your particular machine to scatter the leavening over the bottom of your baking pan before measuring in the other dry ingredients and then the liquids, pour the water or vegetable broth into your bread pan, followed by the canola oil, and break the egg or eggs into it. Add the all-purpose, barley, and millet flours, the brown sugar, and the salt. Scatter the yeast over the dry ingredients, or, if your machine has a separate dispenser for the leavening, spoon it in there.

Use the machine's quick cycle to bake this loaf.

Apulian Bread

To recreate this crusty three- to five-pound Italian loaf, you'd need a really mammoth bread machine, not to mention a coal-fired one. So any comparison of the loaf presented here with the real thing would find it wanting. Still, it's a very good bread, with a silky texture and a crust that somehow manages to be both crisp and chewy. The almost imperceptible sour taste and aroma deriving from the starter used are wonderful. Thick slabs or chunks broken from the loaf are the perfect complement to a hearty stew.

To make the starter, called *biga* in Italy, pour half a cupful of warm water into a glass bowl prewarmed by rinsing in hot water. Add a pinch of sugar and a quarter of a teaspoon of yeast, stir briefly, and let the mixture stand for ten minutes or so in a warm spot, say above a pilot light on the stove, until it looks creamy and bubbly. Then mix in a cupful of flour and another half cupful of water.

This concoction should then be allowed to ferment, covered with plastic wrap, anywhere from six to twenty-four hours or more, the time depending on the temperature. On a really hot day, the starter will tend to ferment very quickly. In a cooler clime, the process may take a full day or so.

The longer the starter ferments, the stronger will be the flavor it imparts to the bread. But there can be too much of a good thing. If the mix separates noticeably and a clear liquid settles to the bottom, it's reaching the outer limits of its serviceability. If the starter begins to turn pink, don't use it. Start a new batch.

You'll find that you have more starter than you need, even for a large loaf of this bread. But the starter freezes well. If you divide the extra into separate portions matching the quantity called for in the recipe and freeze each as a separate block, then all you'll need to do when you decide to make up another loaf of the bread is to remove the premeasured cube of starter from the freezer and give it about three to four hours of room temperature in which to become bubbly again before using it.

SMALL

¾ cup water or vegetable broth
¼ cup starter
1¾ cups unbleached all-purpose
   flour
½ to 1½ teaspoons salt to taste
½ teaspoon active dry yeast

LARGE

1½ cups water or vegetable broth
⅓ cup starter
3¾ cups unbleached all-purpose
   flour
1 to 2 teaspoons salt to taste
1 teaspoon active dry yeast

Pour the water or vegetable broth into your baking pan and add the starter, flour, salt, and yeast. If the instructions that came with your bread machine call for starting with the yeast, however, you'll need to remember to reverse the order of ingredients.

Use the regular full-cycle setting on your bread machine for this loaf, to take maximum advantage of both the starter's leavening power and its distinctive flavor.

7 · Multigrain Breads

THE DAILY BREAD that has been part of my life for as long as I can remember has taken a multitude of forms. Like most children growing up in Europe during and after World War II, I didn't have to be reminded to clean my plate, and the pieces of bread with which I did so were broken from many different loaves. Some of the great variety in taste and texture of the breads of the Old World and beyond has been "rediscovered" in this country only during the past decade or so of culinary expansion. For a long time we were a nation of white bread.

I vividly remember being told stories of the great hungers of the 1800s, when in desperation people made bread of anything flourlike in consistency, including the ground bark of trees. Bread has in fact been made of many things besides wheat flours over the years, and in many shapes as well, from the huge free-form loaves of central Europe to the paper-thin *chappatis* of India.

Bread machines will make neither of those. But these electronic ovens can produce a range of delicious multigrain breads far wider than might be imagined from the instruction booklets accompanying the devices. Richly flavorsome, these multigrain breads served merely with butter are close to a meal in themselves.

Sprouted Wheat Bread

This bread is the sixties and seventies revisited with the nineties grafted on. Our children still remember the sprouter in our kitchen and the young shoots we scooped from it into whatever happened to be in the culinary making. Our sprouting has trickled to an occasional event these days, but the diminutive germinated seeds are still nice in a salad, and they add to this bread a grand nutty taste along with extra nutrition.

The celery seed is right on the cutting edge of health-food enhancement, it turns out. Researchers at the University of Chicago Medical Center have discovered that a chemical constituent of celery called 3-n-butyl phthalide lowers blood pressure and cholesterol significantly. Celery is an old Chinese remedy for high blood pressure as well, so maybe it is especially good for us. In any case, the tiny seeds contribute a refreshing piquancy to the loaf.

The measurement for the sprouted wheat in the recipe is for the dry grains to be germinated, because once they've sprouted, it's difficult to pack them, with all their tangled roots, into a measuring cup. Anywhere from one to three days is required for the roots to reach the preferred length of once to twice the length of the seeds themselves. You'll need to take this into account when planning to bake this loaf.

SMALL
1 cup water or vegetable broth
1 tablespoon olive oil
1 tablespoon honey
1/2 cup wheat seeds, sprouted
1 cup unbleached all-purpose flour
1 cup whole-wheat flour
1/2 cup semolina flour
1 teaspoon celery seed
1/2 to 1 1/2 teaspoons salt to taste
1 1/2 teaspoons active dry yeast

LARGE

1½ cups water or vegetable broth

2 tablespoons olive oil

2 tablespoons honey

¾ cup wheat seeds, sprouted

1½ cups unbleached all-purpose
   flour

1½ cups whole-wheat flour

¾ cup semolina flour

2 teaspoons celery seed

1 to 2 teaspoons salt to taste

2 teaspoons active dry yeast

Pour the water or vegetable broth into your bread machine baking pan and add the olive oil and honey, unless the instructions for your machine call for placing the yeast in the bottom of the pan first thing and incorporating the liquids after the other dry ingredients. Measure in the sprouted wheat, the all-purpose, whole-wheat, and semolina flours, the celery seed, and the salt. If your machine has a separate dispenser for leavening, add the yeast there; otherwise, scatter it over the rest of the dry ingredients.

Set your machine to its rapid-bake cycle for this loaf.

One Rye Bread

This bread is an adaptation of the Czechoslovakian Oder River rye. Among my pleasant recollections is one of a memorable evening spent dining on succulent pork sausages served with grand chunks of that bread and accompanied by the original Budweiser, as brewed in the Czech town of Budějovice.

The bread machine version of Oder River rye owes its present name to the fact that in converting the recipe, I had the best results using one measure of everything. Oh, all right, the recipe does happen to call for one and a half teaspoons of yeast, the standard for almost all the small machine-made loaves I bake, but that's the only exception.

Speaking of small, you'll note that I've included no recipe for a two-rye, or large, loaf of this bread. Increasing the volume of the ingredients seems to create more dough than the machine can handle, despite its size. Try as I might, I ended up with either an unevenly kneaded dough or a straining motor. I did succeed in producing a larger loaf by increasing the liquids disproportionately, but then I didn't have the same fine-textured bread. So this remains a small-loaf-only recipe. It can, however, be baked in a large machine if that's what you have. I guess this is a clear case of good things coming in small packages.

If you don't have any pork sausages handy to go with this bread, try it with herring or a hard cheese or just butter and onions, in the European peasant tradition.

1 cup water or vegetable broth
1 tablespoon canola oil
1 tablespoon unsulphured molasses
1 cup unbleached all-purpose flour
1 cup rye flour
1 cup whole-wheat flour
1 tablespoon cocoa
1 tablespoon dehydrated minced
onion
1 tablespoon caraway seeds
1 teaspoon salt
1½ teaspoons active dry yeast

Pour the water or vegetable broth into your baking machine pan and add first the canola oil and molasses, then the all-purpose, rye, and whole-wheat flours, the cocoa, onion, caraway seeds, and salt. Spoon the yeast into its dispenser if your machine has one; if not, scatter the leavening over the other dry ingredients. Should the directions for your machine specify that the yeast is to be placed in the bottom of the pan first thing, however, you'll need to remember to reverse the order in which you add the liquid and the dry ingredients.

Bake the bread on your machine's quick cycle.

Molasses Rye Bread

This is a sweet, dense rye bread, redolent of molasses, that goes well with cheeses. It's particularly good with the Scandinavian goat cheese *gjetost,* now frequently available in cheese emporiums on this side of the Atlantic.

The bread is unusual for a rye in that it contains bran in addition to the rye flour. The bran, besides contributing to the long-lasting quality of the loaf, adds a stick-to-the-ribs moistness to it. Because of its denseness, the loaf tends to be brick-shaped, with a flat top instead of a rounded one.

SMALL

1¼ cups buttermilk

1 tablespoon unsalted butter or canola oil

¼ cup unsulphured molasses

1½ cups unbleached all-purpose flour

1 cup rye flour

½ cup unprocessed wheat bran

½ to 1½ teaspoons salt to taste

1½ teaspoons active dry yeast

LARGE

1¾ cups buttermilk

4 teaspoons unsalted butter or canola oil

½ cup unsulphured molasses

3 cups unbleached all-purpose flour

1½ cups rye flour

¾ cup unprocessed wheat bran

1 to 2 teaspoons salt to taste

2 teaspoons active dry yeast

Pour the buttermilk into your bread machine baking pan, unless the instructions for the model you have specify that the yeast is to be placed in the pan first and the liquids last, and add the butter or canola oil and the molasses. Then measure in the all-purpose and rye flours, followed by the bran, salt, and yeast. If your machine is equipped with a separate dispenser for leavening, the yeast should be spooned into the dispenser after all the other ingredients have been placed in the pan.

Use the regular baking cycle on your machine for this loaf.

Garlic Pumpernickel Bread

Pumpernickel has a longstanding flavor relationship with molasses and onions. Molasses also helps to give a pumpernickel loaf its traditional dark mahogany color. But the onion has no such secondary function, and so substituting garlic for it does little to affect the bread except to enhance its flavor in a way somewhat different from that of the onion.

This fine-textured, compact loaf is elegant sliced thin and served with cold cuts and a horseradish-spiked mustard. There's nothing subtle here, rather a palette of forceful flavors.

Yes, all of those cups of flour do fit into a one-pound bread machine pan; the loaf is that compact. Lightweight machines such as the DAK and the Welbilt, however, do have problems handling the dough.

SMALL

1 1/2 cups water or vegetable broth
1/4 cup unsulphured molasses
1/4 cup olive oil
2 cups pumpernickel or rye flour
1 cup unbleached all-purpose flour
1 cup whole-wheat flour
2 teaspoons garlic powder or 4 cloves fresh garlic, pressed
2 teaspoons instant coffee, regular or decaffeinated, or Postum
1 teaspoon cocoa
1/2 to 1 1/2 teaspoons salt to taste
1 1/2 teaspoons active dry yeast

LARGE

2 cups water or vegetable broth
1/3 cup unsulphured molasses
1/3 cup olive oil
3 cups pumpernickel or rye flour
1 1/4 cups unbleached all-purpose flour
1 cup whole-wheat flour
1 tablespoon garlic powder or 6 cloves fresh garlic, pressed
1 tablespoon instant coffee, regular or decaffeinated, or Postum
2 teaspoons cocoa
1 to 2 teaspoons salt to taste
2 teaspoons active dry yeast

Unless the instructions for the bread machine you have specify that the leavening is to be placed in the baking pan first, followed by the other dry ingredients and then the liquids, pour the water or vegetable broth, molasses, and olive oil into your pan. Then add the pumpernickel or rye, all-purpose, and whole-wheat flours, the garlic, coffee or Postum, cocoa, and salt. Last, add the yeast, following the instructions given for your particular machine. If the model you have features a separate dispenser for leavening, add the yeast there.

Your bread machine can be set to either its regular or its quick cycle for this loaf.

Brown Rice Amaranth Bread

Did the Aztecs, consumers of amaranth in the ancient days, mill it and use the flour to make bread? Failing a definitive answer to that question, I surmise the tiny grains were too small to mill satisfactorily with the technology of the times.

Today amaranth is used primarily in the form of a hot cereal or sprinkled uncooked over salads to add a pleasant textural contrast. I use it to the same purpose in this loaf, where its high protein and fiber nutritionally complement the brown rice, yielding a loaf that is very nearly a balanced low-fat meal in itself. The bread is full-bodied, nutty, sweet, and superb with smooth flavorsome cheeses like Swiss. It's also delightful simply with butter.

SMALL

1 cup milk, whole or skim

2 tablespoons honey

1/2 cup pecan halves

1 cup semolina flour

1 cup brown rice flour

1/4 cup whole-wheat flour

1/2 cup amaranth seed

1/4 to 1 teaspoon salt to taste

1 1/2 teaspoons active dry yeast

LARGE

1 1/2 cups milk, whole or skim

3 tablespoons honey

3/4 cup pecan halves

2 cups semolina flour

1½ cups brown rice flour
½ cup whole-wheat flour
1 cup amaranth seed

½ to 2 teaspoons salt to taste
2 teaspoons active dry yeast

Pour the milk into your baking machine bread pan, unless the directions for the model you have specify placing the yeast in the bottom of the pan, followed first by the other dry ingredients and then by the liquids, and measure in the honey, pecans, and semolina, brown rice, and whole-wheat flours. Add the amaranth seed and the salt, then spoon the yeast into the leavening dispenser or, failing that device, scatter it over the other dry ingredients.

Bake the loaf on your machine's quick cycle.

Brown Rice Bread

Sometimes the best of breads come about by accident. This is such a loaf. To keep the bread machines humming round the clock when I was experimenting with recipes for this book, I would occasionally leave missives for other family members requesting that they feed the machines' hungry maws in my absence.

Now my notes on bread making, intended primarily for myself, are sometimes not entirely clear to others. "Mrs. K.," my fourth-grade penmanship teacher, who always found my script wanting, would no doubt point out that she'd been right all along about the importance of precision in presentation. For when I left the instructions for a rice loaf by one of the bread machines, I neglected to add the word *flour* after *brown rice*.

Susan, aware of the eccentric nature of some of my experiments, dutifully followed the instructions verbatim. Talk about bombs!

However, the failed attempt also made me think. Although the rice had remained embedded in that particular loaf of bread thoroughly uncooked, resembling so many grains of gravel, instant rice should steam itself nicely in the cooking time allowed by the bread machine's baking cycle. And so it does, producing a truly tasty loaf with plenty of nubbly flavor and a nice texture.

No salt is needed in the recipe, as this ingredient is plentifully provided by the soy sauce.

SMALL	LARGE
1¼ cups water or vegetable broth	*1¾ cups water or vegetable broth*
1 tablespoon canola or olive oil	*5 teaspoons canola or olive oil*
2 tablespoons unsulphured molasses	*3 tablespoons unsulphured molasses*
1 tablespoon soy sauce	*2 tablespoons soy sauce*
1 cup unbleached all-purpose flour	*1¾ cups unbleached all-purpose flour*
1 cup whole-wheat flour	*1¾ cups whole-wheat flour*
1 cup instant brown rice	*1½ cups instant brown rice*
½ teaspoon pepper	*1 teaspoon pepper*
1½ teaspoons active dry yeast	*2 teaspoons active dry yeast*

Pour the water or vegetable broth into your bread machine pan and add the canola or olive oil, molasses, and soy sauce. If the instructions for your machine specify that the yeast is to be placed in the pan first, however, remember to reverse the order in which you add the liquid and the dry ingredients. Measure in the all-purpose and whole-wheat flours, then the brown rice and pepper. Scatter the yeast over the other ingredients in the pan or measure it into its own container if your machine has a separate dispenser for the leavening.

Use your machine's rapid-bake cycle for the loaf.

Millet Bread

Millet is sometimes added whole to breads, the snappy little spheres designed to add a bit of interest to otherwise dull-textured loaves. In this particular bread, however, the millet is used in flour form, with flaxseed adding the snap.

The resulting loaf is a nice nutty-flavored one, sunny yellow in color, with a distinctively patterned crust. Toasted or plain, it's great for summer BLTs.

SMALL

1 cup milk, whole or skim
1 tablespoon unsalted butter or
   canola oil
1/4 cup unsulphured molasses
1 egg
1 1/4 cups unbleached all-purpose
   flour
1 cup millet flour
1 cup uncooked oatmeal (not
   instant)
1/2 cup flaxseed
1/2 to 1 1/2 teaspoons salt to taste
1 1/2 teaspoons active dry yeast

LARGE

1 1/2 cups milk, whole or skim
2 tablespoons unsalted butter or
   canola oil
1/3 cup unsulphured molasses
2 eggs
2 cups unbleached all-purpose flour
1 1/2 cups millet flour
2 cups uncooked oatmeal (not
   instant)
1 cup flaxseed
1 to 2 teaspoons salt to taste
2 teaspoons active dry yeast

Pour the milk into your bread machine pan and add the butter or canola oil, molasses, and egg or eggs. Measure in the all-purpose and millet flours, the oatmeal, flaxseed, salt, and yeast, unless your machine has a separate dispenser for the leavening, in which case add the yeast there. If the leavening is to be placed in the bottom of the baking pan for the bread machine you have, however, reverse the order in which you incorporate the liquid and the dry ingredients.

Bake the loaf on your machine's quick cycle.

Sesame Semolina Bread

Every once in a while, one comes across a loaf of bread that's not simply good, but grand. This loaf qualifies for that accolade. Everyone in the family loves it, and there's never a single slice left over with which to experiment in making a stuffing or dumplings or other entremets.

It's a rather unusual loaf, the semolina flour contributing a soft, silky texture and the sesame seeds a nutty touch. Both those ingredients and the barley malt syrup called for in the recipe are usually available at neighborhood health-food stores. The sesame seeds can generally be bought in bulk there as well, at considerable savings over purchasing them in the small containers found on supermarket spice shelves.

SMALL	LARGE
1 cup water	1¾ cups water
1 tablespoon olive oil	5 teaspoons olive oil
1 tablespoon barley malt syrup	5 teaspoons barley malt syrup
1¾ cups semolina flour	3 cups semolina flour
¾ cup unbleached all-purpose flour	1 cup unbleached all-purpose flour
½ cup sesame seeds	1 cup sesame seeds
½ to 1½ teaspoons salt to taste	1 to 2 teaspoons salt to taste
1½ teaspoons active dry yeast	2 teaspoons active dry yeast

Unless the instructions for your bread machine specify that the yeast is to be placed in the bottom of the baking pan, followed by the other dry ingredients and then the liquids, pour the water into your pan and add the olive oil, barley malt syrup, semolina and all-purpose flours, sesame seeds, and salt. Last, add the yeast, placing it in its own separate dispenser if your machine has that feature.

Set your machine to its rapid-bake cycle for this loaf.

Portuguese Corn Bread

Somehow, corn bread has acquired the image of being as American as apple pie. And indeed the quick-bread version, made with baking powder, may well be. But corn bread is also popular in Europe, particularly in the southern countries.

The recipe given here is for a Portuguese corn bread called *bro*, which, like Anadama bread (whose recipe appears in my first book on baking with the electronic oven, *The Bread Machine Bakery Book*), and the Tex-Mex corn bread featured earlier in this book, uses yeast for its leavening. The loaf is far smoother and less crumbly than the quick corn breads with which so many of us are familiar. Like most corn breads, however, it usually accompanies dishes like stews that are heavy on the gravy or sauce.

SMALL

1 cup water or vegetable broth
2 tablespoons olive oil
1½ cups unbleached all-purpose flour
1½ cups cornmeal
2 tablespoons sugar
¼ teaspoon ground nutmeg
½ to 1½ teaspoons salt to taste
1½ teaspoons active dry yeast

LARGE

2 cups water or vegetable broth
3 tablespoons olive oil
3 cups unbleached all-purpose flour
2½ cups cornmeal
3 tablespoons sugar
½ teaspoon ground nutmeg
1 to 2 teaspoons salt to taste
2 teaspoons active dry yeast

Pour the water or vegetable broth and olive oil into the baking pan of your bread machine, unless the instructions for the model you have specify that the leavening is to be placed in the pan first and the liquids last, and add the flour, cornmeal, sugar, nutmeg, salt, and yeast. In machines equipped with a separate dispenser for the leavening, the yeast should be spooned into its container after all the other ingredients have been placed in the pan.

This is a bread for your machine's rapid-bake cycle.

8 · Memories Are Made of This

EVERY GENERATION HAS ITS MEMORIES of wonderful days gone by. What they all have in common, tucked away somewhere in the lunchbox and picnic section of the recollections, is bread.

An old high-school friend of mine, Geoff, now quite a gourmet, lived a decade of his youth eating nothing but baloney sandwiches on white bread for lunch. For me, the rich European milk breads, along with the anise-flavored loaves of Greece and Morocco, are what evoke the most wonderful times past. There's doubtless a special bread in your memory as well, and you can probably add it to your bread machine's repertoire with a bit of experimentation. Meanwhile, here's a sampling of other memories to bake.

Golden Milk Bread

There's a small bakery down the street from my uncle's house in Vienna. I remember on visits to that city going each morning to pick up fresh rolls, always *handgemacht,* "handmade," for breakfast. The long arm of the industrial age has reached even into the ancient order of bakers, and now most of the little kaiser rolls are shaped by machine. For bread connoisseurs like my uncle, however, nothing will do but the original version, and so some establishments still sell the hand-shaped rolls — for twice the price of the others. To be honest, I can't taste the difference.

The same Viennese bakery carried a golden yellow milk bread that I always found superlative. The owner of the establishment attributed its special flavor to the extra egg yolks and the cream used in place of milk in the recipe. Here it is, adapted for the bread machine.

Should you be wondering what to do with the egg whites left from the baking of this bread, the Viennese answer would be to make meringues, those wisps of sugar and air served with chestnut puree, chocolate, and other wickedly rich dessert delights. But that's a confection for another book. . . .

SMALL

3/4 cup heavy cream
3 tablespoons unsalted butter
1 tablespoon honey
1 egg
2 egg yolks
2 cups unbleached all-purpose flour
1/2 to 1 1/2 teaspoons salt to taste
1 teaspoon active dry yeast

LARGE

1 cup heavy cream
1/4 cup unsalted butter
2 tablespoons honey
1 egg
3 egg yolks
2 3/4 cups unbleached all-purpose flour
1 to 2 teaspoons salt to taste
1 1/2 teaspoons active dry yeast

Pour the cream into your bread machine baking pan and measure in the butter. If you are making the large loaf and using butter still cold from the refrigerator, cut it into chunks before placing it in the pan to ensure its blending evenly with the other ingredients. Spoon in the honey and add the egg and egg yolks, the flour, salt, and, last, the yeast, reserving the leavening for its own container where a separate dispenser is provided for it. If the instructions for the machine you have specify placing the leavening in the bottom of the pan first thing, you'll need to remember to add the flour and salt next, the cream, butter, honey, and eggs last.

Bake the loaf on your machine's quick cycle.

Graham Cracker Bread

Snacks in my grade-school days were almost always a pint of milk and a double graham cracker. My own children eat fried graham crackers, which sounds a little weird until one realizes that what they're doing is crushing the crackers and cooking them in butter, thus creating a graham cracker pie crust without the filling.

The reason the school I attended as a youngster served the snacks it did, and the reason we've never really discouraged the fried cracker munchies, is that graham flour ranks high on the nutritional scale, although I should add that the crackers are far sweeter than the flour Dr. Sylvester Graham first promoted as a healthful replacement for white flour back in the 1800s.

The recipe given here utilizes the readily available graham crackers in lieu of graham flour, which is often hard to find. The loaf, slightly sweet but not overpoweringly so, goes splendidly with roast pork or ham. Also, to return the discussion to the halls of learning, slices of this bread sandwiched together with apple butter make great school lunchbox snacks.

SMALL

1 cup milk, whole or skim

2 tablespoons unsalted butter

2 tablespoons dark corn syrup

2 teaspoons vanilla extract

1³/₄ cups unbleached all-purpose flour

11 double graham crackers (one package)

1 teaspoon cinnamon

1¹/₂ teaspoons active dry yeast

LARGE

1¹/₂ cups milk, whole or skim

3 tablespoons unsalted butter

3 tablespoons dark corn syrup

1 tablespoon vanilla extract

3 cups unbleached all-purpose flour

18 double graham crackers

1¹/₂ teaspoons cinnamon

2 teaspoons active dry yeast

Pour the milk into your bread machine pan and add the butter. If you are making the large loaf and using butter cold from the refrigerator, cut it into chunks before placing it in the pan, to facilitate its blending with the other ingredients. Measure in the corn syrup, vanilla extract, and flour. Toss in the graham crackers, crushing them in your hand as you go, and the cinnamon, and add the yeast as directed for your machine. Remember to reverse the order of ingredients if so instructed.

Use your machine's quick cycle to bake this loaf.

Fluffy White Bread

White bread is everywhere, so why bother to bake it at home? Well, I can think of half a dozen reasons. For one thing, nothing can match the taste of a truly fresh-from-the-oven loaf of bread. And unless you live next to a bakery, nothing can match the aroma, either. Besides, the electronic oven makes it all so easy, there's no real reason not to.

Then there's the matter of ingredients. You know what's in a loaf of bread you've made yourself — and what's not in it. You can limit or eliminate entirely unwanted elements like sugars, sodium, cholesterol, gluten, and certainly such additives as preservatives and "flavor enhancers." But probably the most compelling reason for baking a homemade loaf of old-fashioned fluffy white bread is that it's the kind of bread many of us grew up with — comfort food, they call it.

Here, then, is a homemade bread as simple and light as it is good. For a pleasant surprise, once in a while add a couple of drops of almond, vanilla, or other extract to the dough mix. That barest hint of modification may not be part of the memory, but the unexpected variation may well stir up new dreams.

SMALL

1/2 cup water
1/2 cup milk, whole or skim
1 tablespoon canola oil
a few drops almond, vanilla, or other extract (optional)
2 cups unbleached all-purpose flour
2 tablespoons sugar
1/4 to 1 teaspoon salt to taste
1 1/2 teaspoons active dry yeast

LARGE

3/4 cup water
3/4 cup milk, whole or skim
4 teaspoons canola oil
a few drops almond, vanilla, or other extract (optional)
3 cups unbleached all-purpose flour
3 tablespoons sugar
1/2 to 1 1/2 teaspoons salt to taste
2 teaspoons active dry yeast

If the directions for your bread machine instruct you to place the yeast in the very bottom of the pan, you will need to reverse the order in which you incorporate the liquids and dry ingredients. Otherwise pour the water and milk into your baking pan and add the canola oil, flavoring extract as desired, flour, sugar, salt, and yeast, reserving the leavening for its own separate dispenser if your machine has one.

Bake the loaf on your machine's quick cycle.

Poppy Seed Burst

Poppy seeds are indisputably a matter of taste. A dusting of these slightly bitter decorative seeds over the top of a roll makes a visual statement without much gustatory accent. A large quantity of them, on the other hand, inspires either genuine pleasure or strong aversion.

I well remember my grandmother's strudels. She would stretch the phyllo dough into a paper-thin membrane with her hands and elbows, something I've never been able to accomplish, and fill it with one of a thousand delights — apples, cherries, mulberries, nuts, even cabbage. Then there was poppy seed strudel. Luckily, my father, for whom the very thought of this strudel was enough to arouse ecstasy, would surreptitiously and without fail eat my piece whenever this so-called delicacy was served.

Yet here's a bread I really like that's chock-full of poppy seeds. An attractive, hearty, nutty-flavored loaf, it goes well with venison and robust stews.

SMALL	LARGE
¾ cup milk, whole or skim	*1½ cups milk, whole or skim*
1 tablespoon unsalted butter or canola oil	*2 tablespoons unsalted butter or canola oil*
2 tablespoons honey	*2 tablespoons honey*
1 tablespoon lemon juice	*1½ tablespoons lemon juice*
2 cups unbleached all-purpose flour	*3½ cups unbleached all-purpose flour*
2 tablespoons dark brown sugar	*¼ cup firmly packed dark brown sugar*
2 tablespoons poppy seeds	*3 tablespoons poppy seeds*
¼ to 1 teaspoon salt to taste	*½ to 1½ teaspoons salt to taste*
1½ teaspoons active dry yeast	*2 teaspoons active dry yeast*

Pour the milk into your bread machine pan, unless the instructions for the machine you have specify that the yeast is to be placed in the pan first, the other dry ingredients next, and the liquids last. Add the butter or canola oil, honey, lemon juice, flour, brown sugar, poppy seeds, salt, and yeast. If your machine has a separate dispenser for leavening, spoon the yeast into its slot after all the other ingredients have been measured into the baking pan.

Set your machine to its quick cycle to bake the loaf.

Moroccan Anise Bread

Morocco, home of this bread, is a country of brilliant sunshine, verdant mountains, and vast deserts. The merest whiff of anise drifting past me brings back memories of the once black 1934 Citröen sedan my college friend Abe and I, temporarily diverted from the pursuit of our mortarboards, bought from a certain Ahmad in a Tangiers alley. Some few days later, it expired on the pastel desert beyond the Atlas Mountains, about fifty kilometers from Ksar es Souk, leaving us with but the proverbial bit of bread and water for sustenance. Sample this loaf with lamb shish kebab, and you can't help but hear the *Sheherezade*.

SMALL	LARGE
¾ cup water	*¾ cup water*
½ cup milk, whole or skim	*⅔ cup milk, whole or skim*
1½ cups unbleached all-purpose flour	*2 cups unbleached all-purpose flour*
1¼ cups whole-wheat flour	*1½ cups whole-wheat flour*
1 teaspoon sugar	*2 teaspoons sugar*
2 tablespoons sesame seeds	*3 tablespoons sesame seeds*
1 tablespoon aniseed	*2 tablespoons aniseed*
½ to 1½ teaspoons salt to taste	*1 to 2 teaspoons salt to taste*
1½ teaspoons active dry yeast	*2 teaspoons active dry yeast*

Pour the water and milk in your bread machine baking pan and add the all-purpose and whole-wheat flours, the sugar, sesame seeds, aniseed, salt, and yeast, reserving the leavening for its own separate dispenser if your machine has one. However, if the instructions for the model you have direct you to place the leavening in the bottom of the pan first thing, then you will need to remember to reverse the order in which you add the liquid and the dry ingredients.

Use your machine's rapid-bake cycle for this loaf.

9 · Mix Masters and Other Instant Flavors

CAKE MIXES HAVE BEEN AROUND since the 1930s, but it's only in the last couple of decades that their sales have really taken off. As I heard the story, people considered the original mixes just too easy. It was necessary only to dump a mix into a bowl, add water, ladle the concoction into a cake pan, and bake it. Surely something that simple couldn't be that good.

Then one astute packager came up with the idea of having the consumer add the eggs and milk to the mix. This would lend the customer a certain sense of accomplishment while adding a wholesome fresh image to the product.

In today's hurried lives, I'm not sure much of anything can be made too simple. Assuming you feel the same, here's a clutch of recipes for breads whose flavor derives largely from packaged premixed ingredients readily available on supermarket shelves.

Ranch Bread

This loaf has nothing to do with campfires and chuck wagons along the Chisholm Trail — unless the name of the popular creamy salad dressing used in it is somehow related to the frontier days of the last century, but I've been unable to determine any such relationship. It simply occurred to me while experimenting with recipes one day that creamy salad dressings have all the ingredients of a loaf of bread except the flour and the yeast. So I added them, with quite satisfactory results.

In making the larger loaf, I diluted the dressing with sour cream for a somewhat lighter, milder bread. If you find the flavor of the small loaf overwhelming — some may, although my family liked its piquancy — try using half a flask of dressing and half a cup of sour cream instead of the dressing alone.

Thick slices of the dense, rich loaf just spread with butter make a meal in themselves. The bread is at its aromatic best served as hot from the electronic oven as good slicing will allow. Any leftovers can be diced and toasted for flavorsome croutons.

SMALL

1 8-ounce flask (1 cup) ranch salad dressing, regular or low-fat, or ½ flask (½ cup) dressing and ½ cup sour cream
2 cups unbleached all-purpose flour
¼ cup cornmeal
1 tablespoon dark brown sugar
½ to 1½ teaspoons salt to taste
1½ teaspoons active dry yeast

LARGE

1 8-ounce flask (1 cup) ranch salad dressing, regular or low-fat
½ cup sour cream
3 cups unbleached all-purpose flour
⅓ cup cornmeal
2 tablespoons dark brown sugar
1 to 2 teaspoons salt to taste
2 teaspoons active dry yeast

Unless the instructions that came with your machine call for placing the yeast in the bottom of the pan, followed by the other dry ingredients and then the liquids, put the salad dressing or dressing and sour cream into your baking pan. Add the flour, cornmeal, brown sugar, salt, and yeast, reserving the leavening for its own dispenser if your machine has one.

Bake the bread on your machine's quick cycle.

Wheatena Bread

Hearty breakfast breads can be created from the many multigrain cereal mixes on the market, as I discovered in making the seven-grains loaf for my first volume on bread, *The Bread Machine Bakery Book*. The particular loaf presented here, however, relies on a single cereal for its unusual flavor, and while it's rare that I tout a specific brand, I know of no generic form of Wheatena, the key flavoring ingredient.

An attractive, evenly shaped loaf with a nutty taste and an unexpected snap, this bread should not be limited to breakfast time simply because it's cereal based. All the cold cuts that go well with mustard are nicely complemented by it.

SMALL

1 cup milk, whole or skim

1 1/2 cups unbleached all-purpose flour

1/2 cup uncooked Wheatena

3 tablespoons dark brown sugar

1/8 teaspoon mace

1/2 to 1 1/2 teaspoons salt to taste

1 1/2 teaspoons active dry yeast

LARGE

1 1/2 cups milk, whole or skim

3 cups unbleached all-purpose flour

1 cup uncooked Wheatena

1/3 cup firmly packed dark brown sugar

1/4 teaspoon mace

1 to 2 teaspoons salt to taste

2 teaspoons active dry yeast

Pour the milk into the baking pan of your bread machine and add the flour, Wheatena, brown sugar, mace, and salt. Then, unless the instructions that came with the model you have call for reversing the order in which the yeast and the milk are incorporated into the dough, either scatter the yeast over these ingredients or spoon it into its own separate dispenser if that feature is provided on your machine.

Bake the loaf on your machine's quick cycle.

Spud Bud Bread

Potato bread is one of those great-tasting breads not often made anymore. I suspect its neglect can be traced to the shortage of leftover potatoes in fridges nowadays, what with so many quick-fix dinners being consumed, plus the lack of time to cook up a whole fresh potful of potatoes in lieu of them, all for a mere loaf of bread. But here's a modified Hungarian potato bread that uses instant potato "buds," or flakes, and thus can easily be made any time it's wanted. I like the loaf the traditional way, with caraway. The rest of the family prefer it plain. Bake yours to suit.

SMALL
3/4 cup water
1 tablespoon unsalted butter or
  canola oil
1 1/2 cups unbleached all-purpose
  flour
1/2 cup instant mashed potato buds
1 tablespoon sugar
2 teaspoons caraway seeds
  (optional)
1/2 to 1 1/2 teaspoons salt to taste
1 1/2 teaspoons active dry yeast

LARGE
1 cup water
2 tablespoons unsalted butter or
  canola oil
2 cups unbleached all-purpose flour
3/4 cup instant mashed potato buds
2 tablespoons sugar
1 tablespoon caraway seeds
  (optional)
1 to 2 teaspoons salt to taste
2 teaspoons active dry yeast

Measure the water and butter or canola oil into the baking pan of your bread machine. Then add the flour, instant mashed potato, sugar, caraway seeds if desired, salt, and yeast, following the directions that came with your particular machine for incorporating the leavening, as for some models the order in which the ingredients are placed in the pan should be reversed.

Use the quick baking cycle on your machine for this loaf.

Salsa Bread

Mexican fare, albeit modified and highly stylized sometimes, seems about to become as "American" as pizza, which as found in this country bears equally little resemblance to the Italian original, and salsa is everywhere these days. Now I remember from my youthful travels in Mexico many a tasty meal of *molé* and goat wrapped in corn tortillas. But salsa, that current culinary craze, does not feature in my recollections.

Our kids snack their way through a large jar of salsa in no time. I once jokingly remarked that the saucy stuff would soon replace peanut butter as the spread of choice in our family. It was shortly thereafter that I concocted this loaf.

Tomato orange in color, salsa bread with its distinctive piquant flavor is a good foil for cold cuts in summer sandwiches. Salt is not needed, as there's plenty of spicing in the sauce. Choose the mild, medium, or hot variety to suit your taste.

SMALL	LARGE
1 cup thick salsa	*1²/₃ cups (1 16-ounce jar) thick salsa*
2 cups unbleached all-purpose flour	*3 cups unbleached all-purpose flour*
¹/₂ cup cornmeal	*1 cup cornmeal*
1¹/₂ teaspoons active dry yeast	*2 teaspoons active dry yeast*

Scoop the salsa into your baking machine pan and add the flour, cornmeal, and yeast, following the directions that came with your particular machine for incorporating the leavening, as some machines specify reversing the order in which the ingredients are placed in the pan.

To bake the loaf, set your machine on its quick cycle.

Refried Bean Bread

Instant refried bean mixes are available at most health-food stores these days. Dehydrated flakes of precooked pinto beans seasoned with onion, salt, and spices, they are supposed to be reconstituted with boiling water. However, they also serve admirably as the flavoring agent for a quick and unusual bread.

Cold sliced chicken, mayonnaise, and a sprinkling of fresh cilantro are marvelous sandwiched between toasted pieces of this bread. So are salsa — but of course — and cheddar or Monterey Jack cheese grilled to a melt atop a slab of it, topped just before serving with shredded lettuce and sour cream.

SMALL	LARGE
1¼ cups buttermilk	1¾ cups buttermilk
2 tablespoons unsalted butter or canola oil	3 tablespoons unsalted butter or canola oil
1½ cups unbleached all-purpose flour	2⅓ cups unbleached all-purpose flour
½ cup instant refried bean mix	1 cup instant refried bean mix
1½ teaspoons active dry yeast	2 teaspoons active dry yeast

Put the buttermilk and butter or canola oil into your bread machine baking pan and add the flour and refried bean mix, unless the instructions that came with your machine call for reversing the order in which the leavening and the liquids are incorporated into the batter. Then either spoon the yeast into its own separate dispenser, if your machine has that feature, or scatter it over the other ingredients.

Bake the loaf on your machine's quick cycle.

Teriyaki Bread and Other Flavorsome Rice Oddities

Considering the circumstance of the bread machine's Oriental origins, itself odd enough in view of that vast region's scarcity of breads, I suppose the concept of teriyaki bread is not all that strange. This loaf materialized because I was looking for ways to expand the machine's horizons while staying within the limits of what these electronic ovens do best, which is to bake visually rather similar but gustatorily quite different breads with the barest of effort on their owners' part, when an array of quick-cooking rice dishes on the supermarket shelf caught my eye. I picked up a few.

My initial assortment included teriyaki, broccoli au gratin, and chicken and cheese. Although the contents of the boxes varied from 4.5 to 6 ounces among the sundry brands, I found they could be interchanged quite successfully in the basic recipe given here.

When using these mixes, however, it's a good idea to open the lid of your electronic oven a couple of minutes into the kneading cycle to check the dough. It should be forming into a ball that the mixing blade of your machine can batter around. If the dough is too soft, sticking to the edges of the pan and acquiring a bowl shape, add extra flour a little at a time until the dough rolls up.

The rice grains scattered throughout the baked loaf will be quite al dente, but not more so than they are in some of the upscale restaurant dishes presently in vogue. The firm grains contribute nice contrast and a good crust to the bread.

SMALL

1 cup water or vegetable broth
1 tablespoon canola oil
1 4.5- to 6-ounce box quick-cooking
   teriyaki or other rice mix
1 1/2 cups unbleached all-purpose
   flour
1 1/2 teaspoons active dry yeast

LARGE

1 1/2 cups water or vegetable broth
2 tablespoons canola oil
1 4.5- to 6-ounce box quick-cooking
   teriyaki or other rice mix
3 cups unbleached all-purpose flour
2 teaspoons active dry yeast

Pour the water or vegetable broth into the baking pan of your bread machine, followed by the canola oil and the teriyaki or other rice mix. Add the flour and the yeast, remembering, however, to follow the directions that came with your particular machine for incorporating the leavening; if the yeast is to be placed in the pan first thing, then the water or broth and the oil should be reserved till last.

Use your machine's rapid-bake cycle for this loaf.

Falafel Bread

Falafel, the piquant Middle Eastern fare made from garbanzos, or chick-peas, yellow peas, wheat germ, and spices from the Oriental bazaars, has always been a favorite staple of desert travelers because of the ease with which the lightweight mix could be prepared into a nutritious, protein-rich meal. That same ease of preparation makes falafel an ideal ingredient for bread machine baking. Instead of being reconstituted and rolled into the traditional small balls for nibbling, the falafel mix is simply incorporated into the bread dough. Because the blend is already highly seasoned, no additional salt is needed.

The aroma of this bread while baking, exotic and enticing, makes it difficult to resist pulling the loaf from the electronic oven before the finishing beep. Try a slice slathered with tahini, the traditional sesame seed butter that so often accompanies falafel in the Middle East. The spread can be found in the same Oriental shops and health-food stores that carry the falafel mix.

SMALL

1 cup water or vegetable broth
3 tablespoons olive oil
1½ cups unbleached all-purpose
  flour
½ cup whole-wheat flour
½ cup unreconstituted falafel mix
1½ teaspoons active dry yeast

LARGE

1¼ cups water or vegetable broth
⅓ cup olive oil
2 cups unbleached all-purpose flour
¾ cup whole-wheat flour
1 cup unreconstituted falafel mix
2 teaspoons active dry yeast

Pour the water or vegetable broth into the baking pan of your bread machine, unless the instructions that came with the model you have call for starting with the yeast, in which case you will need to reverse the order in which the liquid and the dry ingredients are incorporated into your batter. Add the olive oil, all-purpose and whole-wheat flours, falafel mix, and yeast. If your machine has a separate dispenser for leavening, spoon the yeast in there.

Set your machine to its rapid-bake cycle for this loaf.

10 · No Gluten, No Cholesterol, and Other No-Nos

O NE PLACE where bread machines really shine is in custom baking for those with special dietary needs. When a loaf of bread is home baked, you know what went into it, so there's no need to worry about the wrong ingredients sneaking into your diet. At the same time, the machines are capable of handling doughs too sticky or otherwise too difficult to work by hand that apart from this hurdle make perfectly wonderful breads. I'm thinking here particularly of gluten-free bread, which at the outset of its preparation, the designation notwithstanding, more resembles a large blob of glue suspiciously like the gelatinous stuff it's supposed to be free of than a normal bread dough.

With the single exception of some kind of liquid, bread lacking any of the ingredients ordinarily considered essential — salt, sugar, even wheat — can be produced with a bread machine. Experiment with whatever a given diet might permit, and chances are you can come up with a good bread, sometimes even a great one like the saltless loaf in this chapter.

Saltless Tuscan Bread

Salt is conventionally deemed as basic an ingredient of bread as flour and a liquid are. Not only does it supply a flavor-enhancing accent to which we've become accustomed, but it slows the action of yeast, inducing smoother and more uniform leavening.

Although rare, saltless breads existed long before our diet-conscious age, in which almost any product can be purchased free of sugar, sodium, or what have you. The reason for the omission of salt in the old days had more to do with matters of finance than with health, however. Salt was a relatively expensive commodity because it was easy to tax.

The tender and flavorsome though saltless loaves of Tuscany on which the recipe given here is based are leavened by a starter similar to the one used in Apulian bread but omitting the pinch of sugar. However, because the Tuscan loaf uses far more starter, it can be baked on your machine's quick cycle.

The starter recipe given here is presented as a small batch in order to simplify visualizing the proportions of the ingredients. However, it can readily be doubled or tripled and frozen in portion-size quantities, to be defrosted three or four hours before needed.

To make the basic starter, pour half a cupful of warm water into a glass bowl prewarmed by a hot-water rinse and mix into it a quarter of a teaspoon of yeast. Let the mixture rest in a warm spot, such as the oven of a gas stove or the rangetop above a pilot light, until it has a creamy, bubbly look, a matter of ten minutes or so. Then, with a wooden spoon, stir in a cupful of flour and another half cup of water.

This mixture should ferment, covered with plastic wrap, from six hours to a day or more. It will ferment quickly in hot weather; in cold weather it may take a couple of days.

If the mixture separates, leaving a clear liquid at the bottom, you may have to discard it. The starter should smell sour and fresh. If it's slimy, it's been left too long.

Starters do vary in consistency and strength as they grow. In some instances you may find that a dough made with the amount of starter listed in the recipe is too stiff for your machine to knead. I've encountered this problem more often with large loaves and oblong pans than in the making of smaller square or round loaves. Check the dough a few minutes into the preliminary mixing cycle, and if it's too firm, add a little extra water.

SMALL

1 cup starter

½ cup water or vegetable broth

2 cups unbleached all-purpose flour

1 teaspoon active dry yeast

LARGE

1½ cups starter

1¼ cups water or vegetable broth

2¾ cups unbleached all-purpose flour

1½ teaspoons active dry yeast

Unless the instructions that came with your baking machine call for starting with the dry leavening, place the starter and water or vegetable broth in the baking pan of your bread machine and add the flour. If your machine has a separate dispenser for the yeast, that's where it should go. If not, scatter it over the flour.

Bake this loaf on your machine's quick cycle.

No-Gluten Bread

O ne doesn't realize the importance of the unseen gluten present in most flours until one tries to make bread without it. Gluten adds a stretchy quality to dough that holds it together as it expands under the pressure of the carbon dioxide released by the fermenting yeast. It is gluten that turns the thousands and thousands of tiny bubbles in the dough into semipermanent balloons — the holes, or open texture, you see when slicing bread.

For those allergic to gluten, bread must include no wheat, oat, rye, or related flours. One is limited to working with rice, tapioca, potato, and other less common flours that without something to stretch them produce an inedible, bricklike bread. To lend elasticity to these glutenless flours, guar gum or xanthum gum is added. Of the two, xanthum gum is the more effective substitute, so I have used it here. A source for xanthum gum is listed at the back of this book.

The dough for this bread is extremely sticky, and I found it did not work well in a large batch. Hence the single small-loaf recipe. The bread is a tad heavy and moist, but for a nongluten bread it has rather good flavor and crumb, especially when toasted.

> 1³/₄ *cups buttermilk*
> 1 *teaspoon vinegar*
> 4 *egg whites*
> 2 *cups brown or white rice flour*
> 1¹/₄ *cups tapioca flour*
> 1¹/₂ *teaspoons dark brown sugar*
> 3¹/₂ *teaspoons xanthum gum*
> ¹/₂ *to* 1¹/₂ *teaspoons salt to taste*
> 4¹/₂ *teaspoons active dry yeast*

Place the buttermilk, vinegar, and egg whites in the baking pan of your bread machine. Add the rice and tapioca flours, followed by the brown sugar, xanthum gum, salt, and yeast. The order in which these ingredients are placed in the pan should be reversed if the directions for the bread machine you have specify that the dry ingredients are to be placed in the pan first, the liquids last.

Use your machine's rapid-bake setting in making this loaf. For the first five minutes or so of the mixing cycle, scrape down the sides of the baking pan with a rubber spatula to make sure the rather soft dough blends properly.

No-Fat Bread

There are many recipes for breads low in fat or at least in cholesterol. This one is altogether fat free except for what little is found in the flour and oatmeal, where it is almost an afterthought to the list of nutrients.

Fats add flavor and tenderness to bread. But flavor can be supplied by herbs or spices, and toughness is not a serious problem in fat-free loaves unless you insist on cakelike softness.

Fats also keep bread from going stale prematurely, and therein lies the real problem with most fat-free adaptations. By the time they've made their way from the baker to the store to your home, they're fit only for stuffing.

A bread machine solves this problem nicely, because you can have a loaf of bread fresh from the oven every day if you like. So for those on a fat-restricted diet, here's a tasty loaf with next to none of the forbidden ingredient. Toss everything needed for it into your bread machine before you go to bed, set the timer, and dream of the fragrant awakening you'll have.

SMALL

1 cup water

1 tablespoon unsulphured molasses

2 cups unbleached all-purpose flour

1/2 cup uncooked oatmeal

1/2 teaspoon dried basil

1/2 teaspoon dried sage

1/2 teaspoon garlic powder

1/2 to 1 1/2 teaspoons salt to taste

1 1/2 teaspoons active dry yeast

LARGE

1 1/2 cups water

2 tablespoons unsulphured molasses

3 cups unbleached all-purpose flour

3/4 cup uncooked oatmeal

3/4 teaspoon dried basil

3/4 teaspoon dried sage

3/4 teaspoon garlic powder

1 to 2 teaspoons salt to taste

2 teaspoons active dry yeast

Pour the water into your bread machine baking pan and add the molasses, flour, and oatmeal. Measure in the basil, sage, garlic, salt, and yeast, reserving the leavening for its own separate dispenser if your machine has one. If, on the other hand, the instructions that came with the model you have call for starting with the yeast, remember to reverse the order in which you add the liquid and the dry ingredients.

Your machine's rapid-bake cycle is the one to use for this bread.

Low-Lactose Milk Bread

Milk bread, that rich yellow European bakery fare so delectable for breakfast, is not exactly high on the list of acceptable foods for anyone with lactose intolerance. Here, however, is a tasty low-lactose version of the bread, using reduced-lactose milk found under the name Lactaid in the dairy cases of many supermarkets as well as in health-food stores. It's so good no one would suspect it of being a special-diet loaf.

SMALL
1/2 cup Lactaid
2 egg yolks
1/2 teaspoon vanilla extract
1 1/2 cups unbleached all-purpose flour
2 teaspoons dark brown sugar
1/2 to 1 1/2 teaspoons salt to taste
1 1/2 teaspoons active dry yeast

LARGE
3/4 cup Lactaid
3 egg yolks
1 teaspoon vanilla extract
2 cups unbleached all-purpose flour
1 tablespoon dark brown sugar
1 to 2 teaspoons salt to taste
1 1/2 teaspoons active dry yeast

If the instructions accompanying your bread machine specify placing the yeast in the bottom of your baking pan, you will need to reverse the order in which the liquid and the dry ingredients are incorporated into the batter. Otherwise, pour the Lactaid into your bread machine pan and add the egg yolks and vanilla extract, followed by the flour, brown sugar, salt, and yeast. If you have a machine with its own dispenser for leavening, add the yeast there.

Use your machine's quick cycle to bake the loaf.

Low-Lactose Whole-Wheat Bread

This is a fine, smooth-textured loaf typical of the milk-based breads, but it uses lactose-reduced low-fat milk instead. The combination of the whole-grain proteins with those of dairy products creates food proteins more complete than those of the grains used separately and more similar to those found in meat and fish. So this is the perfect loaf for the lactose-intolerant seeking to maintain a balanced diet while reducing their intake of animal proteins.

SMALL
1 cup Lactaid
1 tablespoon canola oil
1 tablespoon unsulphured molasses
2 cups whole-wheat flour
1/2 cup unbleached all-purpose flour
1/2 to 1 1/2 teaspoons salt to taste
1 1/2 teaspoons active dry yeast

LARGE
1 1/2 cups Lactaid
2 tablespoons canola oil
2 tablespoons unsulphured molasses
3 cups whole-wheat flour
1 cup unbleached all-purpose flour
1 to 2 teaspoons salt to taste
2 teaspoons active dry yeast

Pour the Lactaid into your bread machine baking pan and add the canola oil and molasses, unless the directions that came with your machine specify that the yeast is to be placed in the pan first, followed by the other dry ingredients and then the liquids. Measure in the whole-wheat and all-purpose flours and the salt. If your machine has a separate dispenser for leavening, spoon the yeast in there; if not, scatter it over the rest of the dry ingredients.

This loaf should be baked on your machine's quick cycle.

11 · Coffee Cakes for the Sweet Tooth

THE LINE BETWEEN BREADS AND CAKES can be mighty fine. My guess is that the difference lies in the frosting. Cakes have it — well, usually, anyway — breads don't. On the other hand, a sweet glaze comes very close to being a frosting, so that's not a perfect divide either. Perhaps you'd call the following coffee cakes.

I guess what really sets coffee cakes apart from other baked goods for me is not only that I do drink coffee with them, but that I tend to dunk them as well, an old Swedish habit I picked up from my Tant Larson. Whatever the nomenclature, and however you eat them, they're tasty delights.

Sour Cream Raisin Bread

Because the dough for this bread is fairly dense, the raisins tend to become smashed, insinuating themselves into the overall texture of the loaf rather than remaining plump islands of flavor in its expanse. If you want your bread replete with whole raisins, you need to wait to add them until the machine has nearly finished kneading the dough. Since I seem never to be around at the right moment for that, I simply accept mushed raisins. And if it's the raisin flavor you're after, this almost cakelike loaf accented with the subtle tartness of sour cream is a lovely addition to any baker's repertoire.

SMALL

1 cup sour cream or yogurt, regular
    or low-fat
1 tablespoon canola oil
1 cup raisins
2 cups unbleached all-purpose flour
1 tablespoon dark brown sugar
1 teaspoon cinnamon
1/2 teaspoon ground cloves
1/2 to 1 1/2 teaspoons salt to taste
1 1/2 teaspoons active dry yeast

LARGE

1 1/2 cups sour cream or yogurt,
    regular or low-fat
2 tablespoons canola oil
1 1/2 cups raisins
2 3/4 cups unbleached all-purpose
    flour
2 tablespoons dark brown sugar
2 teaspoons cinnamon
1 teaspoon ground cloves
1 to 2 teaspoons salt to taste
2 teaspoons active dry yeast

Put the sour cream or yogurt, canola oil, and raisins in the baking pan of your bread machine and add the flour, brown sugar, cinnamon, cloves, and salt. If your machine has a separate dispenser for leavening, spoon the yeast in there. Otherwise, scatter it over the other dry ingredients. However, if the instructions that came with your machine call for placing the yeast in the very bottom of the pan first thing, you will need to remember to reverse the order in which you add the liquid and the dry ingredients.

Bake the loaf on your machine's quick cycle.

Dutch Spiced Ginger Bread

G inger is a key spice in Oriental cooking and, strangely enough, considering the plant's tropical origins, in northern European baking as well. Paper-thin gingersnaps grace the Christmas tables of Scandinavia, and the heavier dark ginger cookies, along with gingerbread, are as Germanic as sauerkraut.

This Dutch loaf, however, is rather different from what many of us have come to know as gingerbread. It is far less sweet, and the flavor of ginger is much more subtle. Fresh from the electronic oven on a cold winter's day, it's a wonderful accompaniment to hot chocolate or Dutch coffee, which is half strong coffee and half chocolate. The open-textured slices, if there are any left over, make great French toast.

SMALL

1 cup milk, whole or skim

1 teaspoon canola oil

1 teaspoon honey

1 egg

2 cups unbleached all-purpose flour

2 teaspoons chopped candied orange peel

1/16 teaspoon cinnamon

1/16 teaspoon ground cloves

1/16 teaspoon ground ginger

1/16 teaspoon mace

1/2 to 1 teaspoon salt to taste

1 teaspoon active dry yeast

LARGE

1 1/2 cups milk, whole or skim

1 1/2 teaspoons canola oil

2 teaspoons honey

2 eggs

3 1/2 cups unbleached all-purpose flour

1 tablespoon chopped candied orange peel

1/8 teaspoon cinnamon

1/8 teaspoon ground cloves

1/8 teaspoon ground ginger

1/8 teaspoon mace

1 to 2 teaspoons salt to taste

1 1/2 teaspoons active dry yeast

Pour the milk into your baking machine pan, unless the instructions for the model you have specify placing the yeast in the very bottom of the pan first thing, in which case the other dry ingredients should be added next, the liquids last. Spoon in the canola oil and honey and break the egg or eggs, depending on the size of the loaf you are making, into the pan. Add the flour, candied orange peel, cinnamon, cloves, ginger, mace, and salt. Spoon the yeast into its dispenser if your machine has one, otherwise scatter it over the other dry ingredients.

Use your machine's rapid-bake cycle for this loaf.

Sweet Greek Bread

Here's a cakelike loaf redolent of the anise of distant Greek isles, perfect for a lazy Sunday morning brunch and daydreaming. The egg yolks lend the bread a golden sunny color, the aniseed its distinctive accent. For more uniform flavor, the aniseed can be ground with a mortar and pestle or in a small electric grinder before being added to the dough. But left whole, the little seeds contribute contrast to both the texture and the taste of the bread.

SMALL

2/3 cup milk, whole or skim

1 tablespoon canola oil

1 tablespoon honey

2 egg yolks

2 cups unbleached all-purpose flour

1/2 teaspoon aniseed, ground if desired

1/2 to 1 1/2 teaspoons salt to taste

1 1/2 teaspoons active dry yeast

LARGE

1 1/4 cups milk, whole or skim

2 tablespoons canola oil

2 tablespoons honey

3 egg yolks

3 1/4 cups unbleached all-purpose flour

1 teaspoon aniseed, ground if desired

1 to 2 teaspoons salt to taste

2 teaspoons active dry yeast

Remember that if the instructions accompanying your bread machine call for the yeast to be placed in the baking pan first, the dry ingredients should be added before the liquids. Otherwise pour the milk into your pan and add the canola oil, honey, egg yolks, flour, aniseed, salt, and yeast. If your machine has a separate dispenser for leavening, spoon the yeast into the dispenser after all the other ingredients have been measured into the baking pan.

Bake the loaf using your machine's quick setting.

Applesauce Bread

Come January or February, when the gardens here in New England are frozen so solid that even parsnips can't be pulled any more, we really begin to long for spring and the white orchards of apple blossoms. But if there are no crisp apples left in the cold cellar, still there's always applesauce. Used in bread, it yields a hearty country loaf fragrant and welcome indeed on a cold winter's morning. Molly's response to it was, "Mmmmm. This is my favorite."

SMALL	LARGE
1 cup applesauce, sweetened or unsweetened	1 1/2 cups applesauce, sweetened or unsweetened
2 tablespoons unsalted butter or canola oil	3 tablespoons unsalted butter or canola oil
1 tablespoon honey	2 tablespoons honey
1/2 cup raisins	1 cup raisins
1/2 cup almonds, coarsely chopped	1 cup almonds, coarsely chopped
2 cups unbleached all-purpose flour	3 cups unbleached all-purpose flour
1/4 teaspoon cinnamon	1/2 teaspoon cinnamon
1/8 teaspoon mace	1/4 teaspoon mace
1/2 to 1 1/2 teaspoons salt to taste	1 to 2 teaspoons salt to taste
1 1/2 teaspoons active dry yeast	2 teaspoons active dry yeast

Spoon the applesauce into the baking pan of your bread machine, unless the directions for the model you have instruct you to put the leavening in first, the liquids last. If you are making the large loaf and using butter straight from the refrigerator, cut it into chunks for more even blending, as it will be cold and hard, before next adding it to the pan. If you are using canola oil, it can be added as it comes from its container. Measure in the honey, raisins, almonds, flour, cinnamon, mace, and salt. Place the yeast in its own dispenser if your machine has one. If not, scatter it over the rest of the dry ingredients.

Use the machine's quick cycle to bake the loaf.

Orange Barley Malt Bread

There's nothing quite like the tang of freshly grated lemon or orange peel, and there are times when I will settle for nothing less in my cooking. But I find it handy to have some citrus oil, available in gourmet shops and by mail order, around as well. It does keep the refrigerator crisper from filling up with unsightly bald lemons and oranges whose flavorful skin has been rasped off. By all means feel free to substitute grated orange or lemon zest for the oil in the recipe given here.

SMALL	LARGE
½ cup heavy cream	*⅔ cup heavy cream*
3 tablespoons barley malt syrup	*¼ cup barley malt syrup*
2 teaspoons orange oil or grated orange or lemon zest	*1 tablespoon orange oil or grated orange or lemon zest*
1 egg	*2 eggs*
2 cups unbleached all-purpose flour	*3 cups unbleached all-purpose flour*
½ cup millet flour	*¾ cup millet flour*
½ to 1½ teaspoons salt to taste	*1 to 2 teaspoons salt to taste*
1½ teaspoons active dry yeast	*2 teaspoons active dry yeast*

Pour the cream into your bread machine baking pan and add the barley malt syrup, orange oil or zest, and the egg or, if you are making the large loaf, eggs. Next add the all-purpose and millet flours, salt, and yeast. Remember, however, to follow the directions that came with your particular machine for incorporating these ingredients; if the yeast is to be placed in the pan first thing, then the liquids should be reserved till last.

The rapid-bake setting on your machine is the one to use for this loaf.

Sweet Almond Bread

O f all the nuts used in cooking, almonds are, I think, the best in bread and pastries. When it comes to cakes, there's nothing like Susan's walnut *gâteau*, which contains no flour, just grated walnuts. In pies, pecans surely reign supreme. But for breads and pastries, almonds have no rival. Try this sweet almond bread and see if you don't agree.

SMALL
½ cup milk, whole or skim
2 teaspoons canola oil
1 egg
1 teaspoon almond extract
½ cup blanched almonds, coarsely chopped
2 cups unbleached all-purpose flour
¼ cup firmly packed dark brown sugar
¼ to 1 teaspoon salt to taste
1½ teaspoons active dry yeast

LARGE
¾ cup milk, whole or skim
5 teaspoons canola oil
1 egg
2 teaspoons almond extract
¾ cup blanched almonds, coarsely chopped
3 cups unbleached all-purpose flour
½ cup firmly packed brown sugar
½ to 1½ teaspoons salt to taste
2 teaspoons active dry yeast

Pour the milk into the baking pan of your bread machine, unless the instructions that came with the model you have call for starting with the yeast, in which case the dry ingredients should be added before the liquids, and measure in the canola oil. Break the egg into the pan and spoon in the almond extract. Add the almonds, flour, brown sugar, salt, and yeast, placing the leavening in its own separate dispenser if your machine has that feature.

Use your machine's rapid-bake cycle for this loaf.

Rum and Chocolate Bread

In my opinion, you can recommend this one for grown-ups," commented Revell. Well, not everything is for twelve-year-olds.

This rich, moist loaf nicely complements a cup of strong, fragrant after-dinner coffee. Try serving thin slices of it spread with softened sweet butter flavored by a drop or two of citrus essence, either lemon or orange, and garnished with a twist of bright peel. The silky texture of the bread harmonizes well with the smoothness of the butter, and the double dose of lemon or orange from bread and spread reinforces the citrus accent.

If you read both of the following recipes, you'll notice that the one for the small loaf uses all cream, the one for the large loaf half cream and half milk. The recipe for the large loaf, however, also lists an egg, whereas that for the small loaf doesn't. These modifications balance out the fat and liquid contents for each loaf so that it will bake properly.

SMALL
3/4 cup heavy cream
1/4 cup dark rum
1 teaspoon orange oil
1/2 teaspoon lemon juice
1 teaspoon grated lemon zest
4 teaspoons chocolate syrup
2 cups unbleached all-purpose flour
2 teaspoons cocoa
1/2 to 1 1/2 teaspoons salt to taste
1 teaspoon active dry yeast

LARGE
½ cup heavy cream
½ cup milk, whole or skim
⅓ cup dark rum
1 egg
1 teaspoon orange oil
1 lemon juice

2 teaspoons grated lemon zest
2 tablespoons chocolate syrup
3 cups unbleached all-purpose
    flour
1 tablespoon cocoa
1 to 2 teaspoons salt to taste
1½ teaspoons active dry yeast

Pour the cream or, if you are making a large loaf of this bread, the cream and milk into the baking pan of your bread machine. Add the rum, and, again for the large loaf, the egg. Then measure in the orange oil, lemon juice, zest, chocolate syrup, flour, cocoa, and salt. If your machine has a separate dispenser for leavening, add the yeast there. If not, scatter it over the rest of the dry ingredients. However, if the directions for your machine specify placing the yeast in the bottom of the baking pan, remember to reverse the order in which you add the dry and liquid ingredients.

Bake the loaf on your machine's quick cycle.

12 · Topping It All Off

NO ONE EVER CLAIMED that the aesthetics of baking with a bread machine beats, or even equals, that of creating the variegated traditional loaves adorning *boulangerie* windows and the pages of artful bakery books. Realistically, the puff-topped cubes or oblongs or cylinders with the grooves along their sides that emerge from the electronic oven are the ugly ducklings of the bread basket. Then again, look at what happened to that creature.

The fact is, these loaves are so tasty they're never around long enough for anyone to spend time contemplating their aesthetic shortcomings. Still, there are occasions when you want to share a loaf with neighbors or company and a bit of festive decoration is in order. Those are the times to put together a quick glaze. Normally a glaze is brushed over a loaf either before it's popped into the oven to bake or when it's pulled from the same, hot and steaming. The latter is really the only option for the baker using a bread machine. I've tried lifting the lid of the machine after the rise cycle to brush on a glaze, and although it can be done, usually, it's chancy, always. Also it defeats the purpose of using a bread machine in the first place. If I'm going to hang around waiting to work on the loaf, why then I might as well bake by hand the old-fashioned way.

The choice of glazes is a matter of personal taste. Oat flakes on oatmeal bread are an obvious and traditional adornment. An apricot jam glaze decorates a milk bread splendidly. Less gracefully would it crown a spinach loaf. Come to think of it, I've never glazed a spinach loaf, and I'm not sure exactly what I would try on that one. An egg glaze with poppy seeds might be nice. So might toasted sesame seeds. Experimenting to discover what tastes and looks best with a given bread is half the fun of adding the finishing touches to a loaf.

Basic Egg Glaze

The most basic of all glazes is the egg glaze. Small seeds adhere to it well and accent the crown of a loaf. Flakes of the grains used in a bread are another option, oftentimes giving a signature, so to speak, to the loaf. Oats flecking the crust of an oatmeal bread or barley flakes the crown of a barley loaf announce the contents of the bread beneath.

> *1 egg*
> *1 tablespoon water or milk, whole*
> * or skim*
> *small seeds for garnish — caraway,*
> * mustard, poppy, sesame — or*
> * grain flakes such as oats or rye*

Break the egg into a small bowl and whip in the water or milk. Then when you take a loaf of bread hot from your electronic oven, close the lid of the machine to keep the interior warm and, using a pastry brush, paint the crown of the hot loaf with this glazing mixture. In the case of a bread that promises to be difficult to shake loose from the pan, knock the loaf out, then slip it right back into the container before proceeding with your glazing.

Sprinkle plenty of the small seeds or flakes you've chosen over the glaze and return the pan to the bread machine to bake the glaze on. In two or three minutes it will have turned to a pretty gloss dotted with the little seeds.

Crunchy Salt Glaze

This one's for pretzel lovers and other salt enthusiasts to add to the darker multigrain breads.

> *1 egg*
> *1½ teaspoons honey diluted with*
> *1½ teaspoons warm water*
> *1 tablespoon coarse sea or kosher*
> *salt*

Beat the egg and diluted honey together in a bowl. As soon as you take your bread from the bread machine, close the lid of the machine to keep the oven warm. Knock the bread from its pan to make sure it will slide out easily after glazing, then put it right back into the pan.

Stir the salt into the egg and diluted honey and, working quickly, brush this mixture over the top of the loaf. You'll need a reasonably stiff pastry brush to lift the salt crystals out of the bowl along with the egg mix.

Pop the pan back into the still-warm baking machine for two to three minutes to allow the residual oven heat to bake the glaze on. When you remove the bread the second time, you'll have a sparkling loaf that looks as if it's covered with tiny diamonds.

Apricot Jam Glaze

Wonderful with milk breads, this glaze is also the natural signature for an apricot loaf. It complements many of the nut breads nicely as well.

> *⅓ cup apricot jam*
> *1 teaspoon water*
> *1 teaspoon lemon juice*

In a small pan, stir the apricot jam, water, and lemon juice together and heat. Once the mixture is hot, brush it onto the top and the upper half of the sides of a loaf of sweet bread removed from its pan but still warm from the electronic oven. Don't brush the sticky glaze all the way down to the bottom of the loaf, or you'll have nothing to hang onto when slicing the bread.

Honey Glaze

Here's a sweet glaze that goes well with chocolate and fruit breads. Triple the recipe, and you can use the leftovers as a spread. When slicing a glazed bread, one never gets enough of the topping.

> *1 tablespoon honey*
> *1 tablespoon lemon juice*
> *1 tablespoon triple sec*

Spoon the honey, lemon juice, and triple sec into a small pan and stir over low heat until warm. Brush the glaze over the top and partway down the sides of your loaf of bread as soon as you've taken it from its pan.

· Sources for Baking Ingredients

MANY SUPERMARKETS now stock specialty flours and other exotic baking ingredients not found on their shelves before. What you don't find there you can often find in health-food stores. But some of us live a considerable distance from such shops, and a few of the rarer flours elude even these retailers. So mail order is a helpful source of ingredients. Besides, the catalogs and pamphlets available from the mail-order houses often contain gems of culinary advice. The following are suppliers I have found helpful in my bread-baking ventures.

Birkett Mills

P.O. Box 440
Penn Yan, NY 14527
Tel. (315) 536-3311

FREE PRICE LIST
NO CREDIT CARDS ACCEPTED

This mill specializes in buckwheat products, carrying flour, stone-ground groats, even seeds for sprouting.

Brewster River Mills

Mill Street
Jeffersonville, VT 05464
Tel. (802) 644-2287

FREE BROCHURE

ACCEPTS MASTERCARD AND VISA CREDIT CARDS

Organic flours and meals are available from this supplier.

Ener-Co-Foods, Inc.

P.O. Box 24723
Seattle, WA 98124
Tel. (800) 331-5222

FREE CATALOG

ACCEPTS AMERICAN EXPRESS, MASTERCARD, AND VISA CREDIT CARDS

This company carries xanthum gum and gluten-free flours.

Jaffe Bros., Inc.

P.O. Box 636
Valley Center, CA 92082
Tel. (619) 749-1133

FREE CATALOG

ACCEPTS MASTERCARD AND VISA CREDIT CARDS

This firm features a large selection of organic grains, flours, and meals.

Kenyon Corn Meal Co.

Usquepaugh
West Kingston, RI 02892
Tel. (401) 783-4054

FREE PRICE LIST

ACCEPTS MASTERCARD AND VISA CREDIT CARDS

Various flours and mixes are available from this supplier.

King Arthur Flour

RR 2, Box 56
Norwich, VT 05055
Tel. (800) 827-6836

> FREE CATALOG
>
> ACCEPTS MASTERCARD AND VISA CREDIT CARDS
>
> *This firm carries all the basic flours along with some un-usual ones. It also carries bulk yeast.*

G. B. Ratto & Co.

821 Washington Street
Oakland, CA 94607
Tel. (800) 325-3483

> FREE CATALOG
>
> ACCEPTS MASTERCARD AND VISA CREDIT CARDS
>
> *This firm carries a wide variety of flours and meals, in-cluding garbanzo.*

The Vermont Country Store

P.O. Box 3000
Manchester Center, Vermont 05255
Tel. (802) 362-2400

> FREE CATALOG
>
> ACCEPTS MASTERCARD AND VISA CREDIT CARDS
>
> *Stone-ground flours and cereals as well as other baking ingredients are available from this firm.*

Walnut Acres

Penns Creek, PA 17862
Tel. (800) 433-3998

> FREE CATALOG
>
> ACCEPTS MASTERCARD AND VISA CREDIT CARDS
>
> *This company carries a broad range of flours, including millet.*

Index